T0285956

TRAUMA

AND

RACE

Micah L. McCreary

TRAUMA
AND
RACE

A PATH TO
WELLBEING

Fortress Press
Minneapolis

TRAUMA AND RACE
A Path to Wellbeing

Library of Congress Control Number: 2023933282 (print)

Cover design and illustration by Brad Norr

Print ISBN: 978-1-5064-8112-8
eBook ISBN: 978-1-5064-8113-5

I give thanks and praises to so many, but specifically:

- *To my Creator, Redeemer, and Empowerer.*
- *To my mother and late father.*
- *To my four living siblings and my two deceased siblings.*
- *To my reconnected maternal family.*
- *To my psychology, academic, and substance abuse communities.*
- *To my individual and family clients.*
- *To my teachers, mentors, and pastors.*
- *To my ministry, seminary, and denominational communities.*
- *To my editors and publisher.*
- *To my daughters and sons in psychology and ministry.*
- *To my BFL and my Little Bop.*

Thank you for the journey. Thank you for embracing my gifts. Thank you for the honor of representing each of you.

CONTENTS

FIGURES

INTRODUCTION

KINTSUGI IS THE ancient practice of repairing porcelain fractures with powder resin mixed with gold. The principle of *kintsugi* is that the repairs to the porcelain are a part of the history of the earthen vessel and must be shown and not hidden. As a child growing up on the east side of Detroit, Michigan, I lived just around the corner from Pewabic Pottery on East Jefferson Avenue.[1] One of my fondest memories is of taking a class there and realizing the healing that occurred when I worked with my hands to fashion a bird or pot from the clay.

What I learned at the Pottery (as we called it) and read in the Bible was that a flawed or broken piece of pottery was to be discarded. On the other hand, *kintsugi* allows the artist to repair the cracked pot and transform it from a broken vessel into a work of art, displaying its scars for all to see. *Kintsugi* serves as a perfect metaphor for my approach to race-based trauma. This book is about counseling with African (Black), Latino/a/x, Native (Indigenous), and Asian Americans, or ALANAs, who face odds that are hard to beat and mountains too high to climb. Not only do they face the difficulties inherent to the experience of trauma, but they do so while experiencing systemic racism. The one exacerbates the other. Thus, any attempt to help or heal by a professional must take into consideration this intersectionality.

To account for the intersection of race and trauma means becoming a trauma-informed counselor. The oppressed are not human objects to be disposed of but precious human beings to be recrafted by the counselor and the Creator.[2] ALANAs who have experienced racial trauma are vessels in need of repair (*kintsugi*), and the trauma-informed counselor works with ALANA clients to empower them in their interactions with race and trauma. A therapeutic blueprint that is equally trauma-informed must be adopted. Following this blueprint addresses the symptoms and causes resulting from the intersection of race and trauma.

Dominic, for example, did not know his Mexican American biological father. The sixteen-year-old lived with his African American mother, but because of his light complexion and curly hair, he identified as Latino or white. Dominic's mother eventually brought him to counseling after his white girlfriend "dropped him for pretending" to be white. He was devastated by the breakup and blamed his mother.

As counseling began, it was clear that Dominic's reaction to the breakup was more serious than he or his mother perceived. His symptoms included dreams and night terrors that were typically associated with traumatic events. Dominic was also avoiding school and "friends" on his football team. Moreover, he was having great difficulty regulating his emotions and reported wanting to kill himself. As counseling continued, Dominic revealed that he had been bullied by teammates since starting high school. For two years he was called "Taco" and "Poncho" even when he yelled at them to stop. He also felt he was denied playing time because of his socio-race. Dominic was blown away when his mother disclosed in counseling that his father had suffered similar night terrors and dreams after his second tour in Vietnam. He and the counselor discussed how the symptoms persisted in their family across generations and were layered by past and current violence and abuse. While Dominic was beginning to realize the impact of the race-based trauma he was experiencing, he was not fully open to delving deeper into the race and trauma issues in counseling.

Dominic graduated high school and joined the military. He served in Afghanistan and Iraq. Upon completion of his tour of duty, he was honorably discharged and returned home and was troubled about his direction in life. He was diagnosed by a Veterans Administration Hospital counselor with post-traumatic stress disorder (PTSD). Over the years, his marriage began to fail and his career began to falter. He then reconnected with his counselor. As before, significant issues of race-based trauma surfaced, and Dominic was now ready to confront the matters of race and trauma. During those sessions, counselor and ALANA client focused on the similarities and differences between Dominic and his father. His father was invited into the sessions, and they discussed the intersections between race and his trauma. In time, Dominic improved his relationship with his wife, finished college, established a successful career, and purchased a home. Dealing with the race-based trauma was critical to Dominic's healing.

Trauma and Race: A Path to Wellbeing is about one psychotherapist's quest to tend the wounds of ALANA clients like Dominic and his family. All cases, stories, and illustrations in this book are composites of the many clinical situations in which this counselor has been graced to work.

Part I

RACE AND TRAUMA

1

SOCIOLOGY

I FELT GOOD as I finished preaching that June Sunday morning. I had been in the flow. It was Pentecost Sunday and "Room for All" Sunday during our denominational General Synod meeting. I preached on the subject "Free at Last" and focused on healing our inherited and internalized family pain and trauma. Using the Song of Deborah in Judges 5:1–18, I raised the complicated question, "What can we do to be free?" This puzzling question was answered by the Parousia, "Celebrate your YHWH, celebrate at your watering places, and celebrate your gifting."

The intersection of socio-race and trauma undergirding that Sunday morning at Hope Church in Holland, Michigan had intensified the worship service and resulted in the Holy Spirit pricking my heart and motivating me to share the struggle and early trauma of my adolescence. The time together proved memorable, meaningful, and enlightening for all. When church attendees affirmed me in the atrium following the service, I sensed their sincerity. I share this story because on that Sunday morning authentic connections were established amid an intersectionality of race and trauma, a place that challenges relationship building.

Facing socio-race and trauma is hard work. In this book, I will use the term "socio-race." The word "race" refers to a social group defined by differences in observable physical characteristics such as skin color and hair. It signifies ethnic, cultural, linguistic, class, and religious differences.[1] It is used to represent differences in people groups that do not exist. I will use the terms "race" and "socio-race" interchangeably but prefer the term "socio-race" over the word "race."

Naming racism often arouses guilt in majority community members who are confronted with data and information regarding the mistreatment of ALANAs by white Americans, or guilt by ALANAs who have survived persecution and consciously regret not being able to "save" others in their socio-racial group. Socio-race discussions that unearth trauma may also produce fear—fear of failure, fear of inadequacy, and fear of isolation. Facing both guilt and fear is daunting. Yet, the trauma and socio-race intersections that Sunday produced a cathartic dialogue between this Black, male preacher and the predominately white, Dutch American congregation. We shared and experienced a refreshing transparency and authenticity.

What transpired that Synod Sunday morning merged my lived experiences and the lived experiences of the Hope Church congregation. Fortunately, the Black preacher was aware of his socio-race and trauma issues, and the white congregation possessed a welcoming, open worldview. Such encounters are rare at historically homogeneous churches. This positive experience was shaped by the pastoral leadership team who had a prophetic focus and a congregation that earnestly pursued justice. That Sunday we were just good people seeking to worship our Creator alongside our neighbors.

Initiating thoughtful socio-race and trauma conversations can produce fruitful encounters around the issues of socio-race, power, and privilege. Unfortunately, these types of engagements can also re-traumatize people with histories of racial trauma. American history bears both productive and harmful socio-race and trauma experiences. As our nation continues to process socio-race and trauma, we are also divided around the issues of truth and freedom. The world's "greatest democracy" is at times the world's greatest hypocrisy. Americans celebrate free speech, yet avoid and often discourage frank dialogue on trauma and socio-race.[2] American history is replete with citizens who resist the reality of socio-race trauma, yet Americans have in the past and continue to participate in socio-race atrocities.

This book invites readers to thoughtfully consider the critical intersectionality of trauma and socio-race. It is a call for Americans to ascend above primal instincts and direct passions to the prodigious traits of hope, faith, and love.

Here in America, socio-race has been used as a weapon, injuring ALANAs and white Americans. This wounding must be metabolized and healed. The resulting trauma from the socio-race wounds leaves devastating scars. This trauma must be transformed into healthy war scars.

Socio-Race as a Weapon

I know about these war scars. At the end of the sixth grade, I was identified as educationally gifted and sent to a middle school for gifted children outside my neighborhood. For reasons discussed later in this book, I pleaded with my mother to allow me to transfer to my neighborhood middle school. Because of my persistence, my mother eventually agreed.

In middle and high school, I especially excelled in physics and math. After the ninth grade, my high school counselor encouraged me to apply for a pre-engineering fellowship program at a technology institute in Indiana. I was awarded the fellowship, so I skipped summer football practice, left my family and friends and the predominately Black cultural environment, and enrolled in the program. I was the only African American there.

I arrived at the school with high expectations and hopes of studying pre-engineering with my peers. Prior to the fellowship I had not taken any courses using computers or computer terminals. I had studied math and physics, but I had not had the opportunity to apply math or science to designing or building. I was a problem solver and a hard worker, so I was surprised when, at the start of the fellowship, I was separated from my peers and assigned the task of building an I-beam and studying its properties. I was never assessed. I was never interviewed and questioned about my experiences and my goals. I was just told that I needed remediation before joining the group. At some point the fellowship staff had determined that I was ill-prepared for the program. I was not allowed to work with the computer terminals and computer programming. I felt angry and attacked. I did not know how to handle this situation. I knew something was not fair, and I perceived the I-beam intervention was beneath me. I was heartbroken and felt targeted.

Embarrassed and feeling as if I had dishonored my school, my counselor, and my family, I decided to leave the program. In a call to my mother, I asked her to send me a bus ticket home. Instead, my mother boarded a bus and rode five hours to the school in Indiana. Upon arriving, she stepped off the bus and hugged me tightly. She looked intently into my eyes and said, "My son is not a quitter!" She then turned around, reboarded the bus, and returned alone to Detroit. From that time on, quitting was never an option for me. I have retreated once or twice, but the lesson I learned that summer was to fight through my socio-race wars. When receiving subsequent wounds from socio-race battles, I have learned to embrace the injuries as life lessons that bring growth and survival.

Initially, I assumed that my story was unique, but over the years many of my friends and colleagues spoke of their racial wounds. My best friend in graduate school, a first generation Asian-Indian American woman, shared that several white teachers discouraged her from maximizing her giftedness in science and math as a young student. Over the years, Black- and brown-skinned people shared again and again the numerous socio-race injuries they have had to overcome.

Racial attacks against ALANAs can be subtle and covert, as well as hostile and overt. ALANAs are frequently told they are not good enough and will not succeed in education, business, or life in general in America. American-born ALANAs are told, "If you don't like it here [in America], go back to your own country." ALANAs are negatively stereotyped—individually and corporately ascribed as being of low intelligence, and often labeled as dirty, violent, lazy, criminal, sexually promiscuous (male and female), and disposable.

A powerful archetype of socio-race as a weapon is "the N-Word." This word has had a powerful impact on the American socio-race experience and exerts great influence in racial group interactions. The N-Word affects all Americans—Black, white, and others—in complex, negative ways. It is both a culture bomb and a culture capsule. The N-Word derives from an ethos that seeks to oppress, subjugate, and humiliate Black people into a people of nothingness. The N-Word lives beyond time and scope. It is a word that grew from the American socio-race experience but has eclipsed earlier socio-race practices. Socio-race is used to classify, categorize, differentiate, and prioritize one people among many and thus the N-Word is a complex tool of separation, oppression, and categorization. It is a multifaceted expression used to consciously differentiate people groups based on observable physical attributes. This group differentiation based on visible characteristics empowers the N-Word, reinforcing white people's creation of an American racial hierarchy.

The N-Word is an awful and awe-filled word. Yet, it is a word that is affectionately used in Black culture and among Black subgroups. The N-Word allows Black people to differentiate their Black people from other Black people. Said at the right time with the right inflection, the N-Word may create Black community space. But even when some Black people use this word affectionately, it is still a word that harms other listeners, both ALANA and white. The N-Word exists in two totally different domains. One domain includes only Black people, and the other separates Black people from one another. That is, Black people use the N-Word to differentiate in-group and out-group membership. The term embodies the concepts and beliefs about Black people in American society. It promotes intellectual violence against Black people. The N-Word is an outward expression of internal ideas and notions, justification of oppressive behaviors, and support for an oppressive social system.

The N-Word is just one weapon used in our socio-race conflicts. A more hideous, bone-breaking socio-race weapon would be lynching. The lynching of Black people in America stands as a hideous and barbaric example of socio-race as a weapon. After enduring years of suffering under American slavery, Black suffering did not end after Blacks were "emancipated." Black people then were confronted with lynching as an evil, extralegal, community-sanctioned act of violence. Lynching became an act of mob violence and torture directed at Blacks after and because of the 1867 Reconstruction Act.[3] Following the Civil War, Congress sought to govern the Southern states more efficiently by organizing ten of the eleven former Confederate states into five military districts. These new government entities granted newly emancipated Black men legislative authority and American citizenship. Among Black people, Reconstruction is remembered as a period of accomplishment and restoration. But it also ushered in an era of torture and hatred that trapped the Northern government and Black survivors.

Governmental failure and atrocities against Blacks in America is not a recent reality. In his book on General Ulysses S. Grant, biographer Ron Chernow writes about General Grant's significant achievement around the end of the war and subsequent accomplishments. He chronicles Grant's campaign against and defeat of the Ku Klux Klan in the early 1870s.[4] However, this victory was brief and led to the monster of oppression (Black laws and Jim Crow segregation) and the persistence of a spirit of white supremacy that resisted the Civil War's outcomes and forced the nation to retreat from Reconstruction's lofty aims. Even the Fifteenth Amendment, which gave Black Americans the right to vote, and the 1875 landmark civil rights legislation, which outlawed racial discrimination in public accommodations, was not enough to protect Black survivors from the hatred and subjugation manifested in lynching.

White southerners conceptualized and envisioned themselves as redeemers of the South: they would save the South from Black empowerment, and they worked to free themselves from federal control. Twenty years after the 1867 Reconstruction Act was passed, it was rescinded, and federal troops were removed from the South. With their departure, an evil more hideous than slavery took hold. To put it simply, Blacks in the South were terrorized. According to historian Joel Williamson, during and after Reconstruction "Blackness alone" was justification and license to shoot, beat, rob, and kill Black people.[5] From the late nineteenth century and early into the twentieth century, an average of two or three Black southerners were hanged, burned at the stake, or quietly murdered every week. Between 1882 and 1968, it is estimated that 4,742 Blacks met their deaths at the hands of lynch mobs.[6] Lynching was not just the act of hanging. Lynching became an event of slow, methodical, sadistic torture and mutilation. This form of violence against Blacks in America was given labels such as "Negro Barbecues" and "Nigger Hunts."[7] There were even sadistic racial caricatures of mutilated Blacks placed on exhibition and sold as souvenirs and postcards, symbolizing and reminding everyone of white power.

Black codes were used by the criminal justice system to force Black people back into slavery.[8] Southern constables and keepers would approach Black men on the street under the racial statutes and conventions of the South and demand that the Black men had the money to prove their right to freedom. The statute stated that a Black man traveling alone could be arrested and charged with vagrancy. Admitting one had no money or no job was to give the constable an excuse to use his official authority to jail the Black man and then hire him off to the mines, factories, or chain gangs.[9]

The accepted and inevitable violence and reenslavement of Black people in America has had a powerful effect on the psychology and sociology of ALANAs, particularly African Americans. Whites commanded the total subordination of Black, and the violence of that time (often referred to as Jim Crow) was so hideous and gripping that it remains an oxymoron to the promise of America realized by European immigrants.

In response to this system of oppression that operated openly with governmental permission and support in the South, many Black people headed north. Isabel Wilkerson describes this great migration in her book entitled *The Warmth of Other Suns*.[10] The title of Wilkerson's book comes from the pages of the unrestored edition of *Black Boy* by Richard Wright:

> *I was leaving the South*
> *To fling myself into the unknown. . . .*
> *I was taking a part of the South*
> *To transplant in alien soil,*
> *To see if it could grow differently,*
> *If it could drink of new and cool rains,*
> *Bend in strange winds,*
> *Respond to the warmth of other suns*
> *And, perhaps, to bloom.*[11]

The poem about migrating north is so real to many ALANAs. I still remember the stories of how my grandfather had to flee the South after a violent confrontation with a white man. The racial violence of the nineteenth century has contributed significantly to the current inequality of educational resources, the propagation of pseudo-scientific theories of socio-race, and the widespread criminal inequities in the justice system. Volumes of books and resources exist that discuss racial violence in greater detail. What is of concern here is how the weaponization of socio-race and socio-race violence manifests as trauma.

The weaponization of socio-race has been far reaching, including into education. Professor Claude Steele of Stanford University conducted a study of ALANA students attending the University of Michigan in the 1980s. He discovered that students who felt the pressure to represent their racial group experienced anxiety during testing that resulted in diminished performance in these "socio-race" identified situations. Steele found that when Black students were told that their racial group performed equal to or above the performance of students in other racial groups, the Black students' performances were not affected in either a positive or negative direction. When Black students were told that their racial group performed poorly compared to other racial groups, their performance in those situations diminished. In summary, the pressure to represent one's socio-race, when one's socio-race is negatively portrayed, results in poorer performance, often resulting in anxiety disorders and depression. Professor Steele labeled this phenomenon "Stereotype Vulnerability." Steele continued to investigate the stereotype vulnerability premise with other students of color and women. He found that vulnerability to the stress of stereotypes occurs in socio-race and gender groups. When socio-race and gender are presented in a negative way, they become weapons that attack the psyche, engendering negative performance due to the internalization of negative messages.

Given that socio-race impinges on our psyches, we must deepen our public conversations from narrow perspectives of socio-race as a Black and white issue to a broader social construct that includes conversations and analyses inclusive of place, such as ghettos, ethnic enclaves, suburbia, and urban gentrification. This issue is not a simple matter of political correctness but a problem of suffering and disenfranchisement due to the racialization of our cities that has resulted in the suffering of ALANAs for centuries. We must remember that the concept of "lifting oneself up by one's bootstraps" was introduced into our language as a metaphor for doing the impossible. Therefore, we weaponize socio-race by blaming ALANAs for not being strong enough to move from the reservation, barrios, slums, or inner city— for not assimilating into American culture.

American culture continues to blame the victim and characterize ALANAs who complain or resist victimization as angry, hateful, and resentful. For example, our current "get in your face" climate portrays Black protestors as rioters and looters, with no sensitivity to the trauma underneath the protest.

Conceptualizing socio-race in America as a purposeful weapon used to destroy the humanity of ALANAs may be either challenging or confirming, depending on one's lived experience. The American dream demands that, no matter what one's social-political orientation, our society must confront the history of rape, genocide, relocation, repatriation, lynching, manifest destiny, mass incarceration, redlining, and other systemic atrocities that have marginalized and prevented ALANAs from achieving true freedom and liberty in America. It is important that racial equity and restoration not occur out of shame or guilt. The wounds of socio-race that have resulted from the use of socio-race as a weapon must be attended to in order to obtain wellness. Unattended wounds rot and become infected. It is important that our restorative efforts dispense with the tradition of blaming the victims and perpetuating new systems of oppression because of fear, sympathy, or a desire to maintain control and status.

We must discontinue the practice of using socio-race to divide and conqueror neighbors and perpetuate false narratives of superiority and inferiority. One method used to foster division instituted in the 1960s was the myth of Asian Americans as a model minority. This myth was manufactured as a racial attack against both Asian Americans and Black Americans in response to the 1960s civil rights and Black Power movements and was a systemic "finger wagged" at Black Americans as they fought for equality. Moreover, it was a tool used to silence the voices and protests of Asians in America who had endured a long history of anti-Asian socio-race violence. For over one hundred years Asians had been the targets of hate, but ironically, in the 1960s, they became the "perfect model" of what racial minority groups in America could be. Forget that Asians were accused of stealing white jobs in the 1850s. Ignore the 1854 ruling of the California Supreme Court that ruled Asians could not testify against white people in court. Overlook the Rock Springs Massacre of 1855, the Chinese Massacre of 1871, and the Chinese Exclusion

Act of 1882. Never mind the Japanese Internment during World War II, which we justify with a qualified apology while continuing to blame the Japanese for the demise of the American automotive industry and loss of American jobs. But, starting in the 1960s, it was proclaimed and pretended that Asian perseverance, strong work ethic, academic success, and allying with whites gives legitimacy to minority success in America. Simultaneously, the myth blamed Asians for the struggling American economy and stereotyped Asians as lusting after white American culture. It is time that we remove our blinders of the intersection of socio-race and trauma. We must label these myths and practices as oppressive tools used to drive a wedge between different racial groups and within the Asian groups.

The reality is that this wonderful country we love is not perfect. Americans have used the weapon of socio-race against ALANAs through violence, policies, laws, education, and myth. We have created and participated in racial violence of neglect, denial, and force. But we must not lower our heads in helpless immobilizing shame. We must raise them in unity and seek communality. From the very beginning of our nation, America has been embroiled in socio-race wars. An examination of the *Encyclopedia of Race and Racism* revealed there is no entry for the word "race."[12] Rather, race is explored as a construct from several perspectives. There are nine essays on various types of racism and eight entries on racial formation. There are also individual essays on race riots, racial profiling, biased policing, and racial purity in the United States. Encyclopedia editor-in-chief Patrick L. Mason does not offer an entry on race but does provide a definition in the introduction. Mason defines race as "referring to social groups partially and inconsistently defined by differences in observable physical characteristics such as skin color and hair, but it also signifies ethnic, cultural, linguistic, and religious differences that animate persistent conflict between social groups."[13] He suggests that investigations of race be comprehensive and systemic.

As an American psychologist, professor, and pastor who is Black, I have counseled, consulted, taught, and preached about socio-race for decades. By necessity, I conceptualized socio-race as a part of my life and survival. For years I have presented socio-race as a tool to be mastered to eradicate the harm of century-long attacks, manipulations, and categorizations against ALANAs. Socio-race is one instrument to use to debunk bias-based American pseudoscientific investigations of human inferiority and superiority. At some point, on an unconscious level, I learned that socio-race was being used as a weapon against ALANAs. From my own experiences—with redlining; the ghettoization of Detroit; family migration from the South; stereotyping; subtle and covert racial attacks; hostile and overt attacks; politicization of socio-race, racial bias, and socio-race prejudices—it was evident that socio-race was being weaponized not just in my life but throughout America.

Whether from being classified and categorized as inferior or being called the N-Word while jogging or being stopped by the police for "driving while Black" in a no N-Word community, I have come to understand and conceptualize socio-race as a tool designed or used to inflict bodily harm, apply mental oppression, and maintain racial caste systems against people of color.

Trauma as a Result

A sentinel memory that stands guard over my life arose from the Detroit Revolts in 1967 and 1968.[14] Since then, I have watched movies of the Detroit Revolts and read books detailing the devastation of those long, hot summers of social unrest. However, the memories of greatest impact are those rooted in my lived experiences. I remember my father placing my six siblings and me in a bathtub to keep us safe. I remember the National Guard's military machinery rolling down Jefferson Avenue and the burned homes and businesses on Mack Avenue near my grandmother's home.

At the time of the 1967 Detroit Revolt, our father was a supervisor for the sanitation department. He was also a veteran of the Korean War and a pastor of a storefront church. I loved the father I had before the revolts—the "before-the-revolt" dad is the dad I proudly walked like, looked like, and carried his middle and last names. After that summer, our father changed. Something about the violence broke him. He became a shell of the man I had admired. My father was broken and despondent.

What my siblings and I did not understand then was that the Detroit Revolts triggered a traumatic memory in our father that led to depression, drinking, gambling, and eventually abandoning his family and his home. The loss of this wonderful husband, father, son, pastor, and community anchor was a personal hell for us that paralleled the hell in our city. Unbeknown to us was the fact that nearly 160 racial revolts occurred across the country during the summer of 1967. What we did know was that people close to us were killed and injured in the Detroit Revolt. We knew that the man we loved the most died socially, spiritually, and psychologically.

As a family we struggled for years after this ordeal. Our father's mental health crisis and subsequent abandonment was emotionally painful and traumatizing. Several of my siblings grew into adults who fled conflict and avoided pain. Others surrendered to the crumpling city infrastructure and rising underground economy. Still others made strides to do better than our father by any means necessary. It was a painful and traumatic era in the life of our family.

Reflecting on my own response to the community and family trauma I experienced, I realize the truth and power of Viktor Frankl's take on stimulus and response. Developing this concept from the experience of Nazi Holocaust concentration camps, Frankl suggested that after every stimulus there is a pause that can be used to contemplate our response prior to making it. This powerful coping suggestion has become an effective tool for me.

In 1991, I discussed this stressful childhood experience surrounding the Detroit Revolts with my graduate school colleagues. As a result, Slavin, Rainer, Gowda, and I proposed expanding the standard stress and coping model to incorporate culture.[15] We based our work largely on the model of stress and coping developed by Lazarus and his colleagues.[16] The Lazarus et al. model included five major components: the occurrence of a potentially stressful event; primary cognitive appraisal; secondary cognitive appraisal; implementation of a coping strategy; and physical and mental health outcomes (see Figure 1.1). Our model sought to include a few culture-relevant factors that seemed useful in organizing available information about the effects of cultural factors on human experiences.

In this stress and coping model, an event includes both major and minor life events. It is during primary appraisal that the event is evaluated to determine whether it presents a threat. In secondary appraisal the individual evaluates his or her resources and options to handle

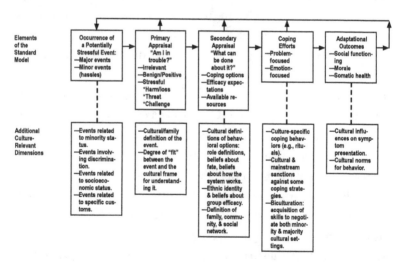

Figure 1.1. Multicultural model of the stress process. Source: from L. A. Slavin, K. L. Rainer, M. L. McCreary, and K. K. Gowda, "Toward a Multicultural Model of the Stress Process," *Journal of Counseling and Development* 70, no. 1 (September 1991): 156.

the event. Here the person or the system evaluates based on available coping resources and determines if the event is harmful, threatening, or challenging. Stress is therefore conceptualized as an inherently interactive phenomenon. No one event is universally stressful. Attention must be allotted to the meaning the individual or system assigns to the event.

In the Lazarus and Folkman model of stress, after an event occurs and is appraised (as primary and secondary), the individual then reacts to the stressful event with a problem-focused or emotional-focused coping response. This response can be conscious or unconscious, as well as effective or ineffective. Our coping responses then lead to our outcomes, and outcomes (behavioral and emotional) can be either adaptive or maladaptive. Stated differently, our mental wellbeing is like a container. Life challenges and stressors from any aspects of our lives are all events placed into the container. If the container overflows, we then attempt to cope with the overflow. Successful self-care is the equivalent of getting help or acquiring the skills to manage the overflow. The more we manage our overflow, the better we function. Maladaptive outcomes occur when we cannot handle the overflow of our emotional containers, when we are emotionally overwhelmed and unable to adapt to the current stressors. When this process continues, persists, and intensifies, we become unwell and can experience mental health issues, such as depression and anxiety. Being unwell does not mean we do not care for ourselves. It means the container is outside of our control and out of control.

Stress and coping models are predicated on the notion that people typically have the resources to respond effectively to life stress and life stressors. Further, the models assume that, with the appropriate resources, normal people will be able to cope with everyday stress and extraordinary life stressors. As the Yerkes-Dodson law proports, our performance, to a point, is improved with increased mental and physiological stress.[17] However, trauma connected to socio-race can perpetuate the overflow of the human container by breaking down our abilities to cope with stress. Socio-race trauma is a reaction to actual life events. It is the perpetual stress resulting from the loss of safety, social unrest, employment concerns, illness, neglect, and abuse that are based on complexion and skin color.

Trauma is more than an emotional and behavioral response to a stress-related difficulty. Most mental health professionals suggest that it is the accumulation of stressors and the maladaptive response to the stressors that result in a trauma experience. Traumas are a mixture of the biology, psychology, sociology, and spiritual aspects of humans remaining in survival mode even when the person is no longer at risk or in danger. The ensuing trauma response, typically a fight, flight, or freeze reaction, when a sudden release of hormones during times of acute stress activates the body's sympathetic nervous system, is an evolved survival response used by the body to protect itself from harm in threatening situations. The sympathetic nervous system then arouses the adrenal glands, which trigger the release of catecholamines (a category of neurotransmitters).

For a stress experience to be diagnosed as a traumatic one, it must evoke in the individual or group what would be considered a significant symptom of distress to most people or groups.[18] Trauma that persists over generations has been termed "historical trauma." As a psychologist and pastor, I prefer the term "soul wound." A soul wound occurs when there is an internalized injury of the mind, body, and spirit that offends one's dignity, violates individual and corporate rights, and sustains losses in value or reputation and is compounded by the fact that the injury (trauma) occurred at the personal, community, and collective levels. This soul wounding or historical trauma is cumulative and can be intergenerationally transmitted. Compounded over generations, these injuries can be internalized. If this trauma is unresolved, it becomes more severe over time. This trauma involves the recognition that horrifically violent experiences inflicted on individuals in the past result in unhealthy outcomes that are passed on to one's offspring. In my clinical practice, I have seen this soul wound morph into healthy and unhealthy cultural distrust.

A soul wound can also destroy familial attachment bonds, which are critical to developing closeness, havens, and secure family/community bonds. An attachment bond is the emotional connection formed by wordless communication between a parent and an infant/child (see Figure 2.1). There are four possible attachment bonds between the infant and caregiver: secure, avoidant, ambivalent, and disorganized.

The forming of a secure attachment bond creates a positive attachment to others and to the self. Attachment bonds are considered critical in reducing anxiety and handling loss. Without a secure attachment bond, or because of an attachment injury, trust is difficult to obtain. Additionally, strong and healthy relationships are nearly impossible to maintain without creating secure attachments that allow people to be vulnerable and buffer stressful situations, hopefully preventing them from becoming traumatic.

Returning to the Detroit Revolts and my father's trauma, I realized that it was not the events themselves that created the trauma. It

Attachment Table: SAAD

	Positive Other	Negative Other
Positive Self	**Secure Attachment**	**Avoidant Attachment**
Negative Self	Ambivalent Attachment	Disorganized Attachment

Figure 2.1. Secure, Avoidant, Ambivalent, and Disorganized (SAAD) attachment chart. Source: created from Tim Clinton and Gary Sibcy, *Attachments* (Brentwood, TN: Thomas Nelson, 2002), loc. 24, Kindle.

was my father's conceptualization and construction of a reality induced by the accumulation of stressors that caused his demise. The haunting memories of his service in the Korean War, the pressure to provide for his growing family, the existential struggle surrounding his faith and spiritual practices, and the vulnerability of life events in 1960s Detroit all worked in synchrony to bring this dignified man to his knees. Our father's accumulated anger, shame, and feelings of isolation resulted in his breakdown after the destruction of his world. The revolts during the summers of 1967 and 1968, born from years of Black American neglect and abuse, triggered his painful Korean War memories, resulting in his traumatic response.

This first-hand experience in Detroit taught my siblings and me that the so-called riots were social revolts. The revolts in Detroit and other urban cities in 1967 and 1968 occurred in the context of the civil rights and Black Power movements, and were internal and external wars fought by subjugated and oppressed Black Americans demoralized by the acts of violence, brutality, and abuse perpetrated by the police. The revolts were overt acts of defiance and challenge to the established political order of that day, including a reaction to and against both police brutality and political actions that created, maintained, and perpetuated a separate and unequal social system. If white Americans had reacted in that manner, their actions would have been chronicled as self-protective.

Do not misunderstand this analysis of socio-race and trauma. This is not a cry for pity, blaming the victims, or blaming the system. This book is written to help readers comprehend the components and intersectionality of trauma and socio-race on ALANAs, an understanding that is critical to our ability to heal ourselves and others and be made whole.

Many of my ALANA clients perceive the power of ALANAs worldwide, but they feel ALANAs in America keep taking small steps forward and then are pushed a giant step backward. This perception creates a troubling trajectory for many of my ALANA clients, who are shocked, angered, bewildered, and triggered by prejudicial actions toward them. Thus, the call from ALANAs for liberation and retaliation comes after many steps backward.

Their calls for freedom must not be ignored. When these traumas are ignored or treated inhumanely, they morph into painful stagnation that is perceived as a backward step. But steps backward or forward must not be perceived as missteps. The steps of ALANAs must be viewed through the lens of the process. They stand on the shoulders of ancestors who also struggled to advance against oppressive acts. The ALANA client must not dishonor the ancestors by wallowing in discontent, but glory in the opportunity to join the battle for racial justice. Steps built on generations of abuse and years of neglect and mistreatment must be conceptualized as steps toward progress and freedom. I recommend a pause and assessment of life and life's situations after either an advance or a setback. This pause, before responding, will enable the responders to contemplate assent and descent and allow us to effectively alter the path. The more we pause and sidestep during the challenges of life, the more opportunities we create to reevaluate and plan our moves forward.

To sidestep the problem is not to avoid it, but to conceptualize and navigate around it. Sidestepping is a strategy to assess, adapt, and then advance. For example, the sacrificial deaths of John and Robert Kennedy and Martin Luther King Jr. in the 1960s were a serious pause for our nation. The Kerner Commission established by President Lyndon Johnson and the Commission's bestselling report about the revolts of 1967 and 1968 was a sidestep for the president and the country. The Supreme Court election of Thurgood Marshall (the first Black justice) and the election of the first African American mayor (Carl Stokes in Cleveland, Ohio) were small steps forward in the fight for human rights. These types of social markers are indicators of a shift in the political landscape that promise a systemic and structural uplift for ALANAs trapped in the desert of second-class citizenship. These signs of hope are needed. Critical to this book is the fact that racial traumas, such as my father's breakdown and the Detroit Revolts, are triggered by unjust actions and behaviors, particularly systemic oppression and mob-led violence and brutality. This type of racial trauma requires freedom fighters, allies, and accomplices to galvanize, separately and collectively, around socio-race issues and trauma issues.

Racial prejudice, discrimination, and systemic oppression have become common terms used in our culture. Interpersonal and intrapersonal socio-race violence demeans and degrades the bodies, psyches, and communities of ALANAs. It hurts and harms in deeply painful ways. Since the 1970s, the movement to counter affirmative action, social advancement, Black power, and the integration of ALANAs into American society has been minimized and overlooked. This socio-race and trauma experience of ALANAs around the world has been a culture war with many casualties. However, American society has conveniently neglected and failed to address the individual pathologies and collective societal illnesses that lie beneath the abuse, hate, and rage against ALANAs. Instead, America has promoted and proclaimed to the world American superiority and portrayed itself as a society that embraces equality. This hypocritical narrative of America as the home of the brave and free, as a nation with unlimited opportunities for industrial agency and social advancement, is celebrated and proclaimed by many and is a reminder of generations of abuse by others.

My psychological assessment of this phenomenon is that America continues to defend itself and its majority constituency, while fooling much of the world, using a reaction-formation defense mechanism. America continues to respond to its anxieties and negative unacceptable emotions by exaggerating the direct opposite. It realizes that it has been unjust and inequitable to its citizens of color. It knows it has not been the home of the brave and land of the free for ALANA citizens, so America loudly proclaims the opposite of what it is. America unjustly incarcerates Black citizens while praising the success of Black citizens who "pulled themselves up by their bootstraps." It celebrates the Servicemen's Readjustment Act (GI Bill), while redlining Black servicemen (GIs) from purchasing houses in white communities.[19]

Regardless of the hypocrisy and frailty of our progress and happiness, America has pressed on as a nation continuing to claim to be the home of the brave and the land of the free. Americans justify the neglect of and refusal to intervene on behalf of the poor and oppressed in our country and in the world by claiming that "those people" rioting, living in ghettos, and committing crimes are only getting what they deserve. These veiled socio-race excuses are not new. Our nation conveniently forgets that for centuries throughout Asia, Europe, Africa, South America, Australia, the Mediterranean, and North America colonizers have used socio-race as a weapon of oppression. Colonizers conveniently and politically ignore the physical and psychological trauma of people who are systematically and forcefully exposed to degrading acts of violence and neglect that occur simply because of observable physical characteristics such as skin color and hair.

The struggle for freedom and equality for the oppressed, neglected, traumatized, and marginalized existed long before 1619, when the first African prisoners were enslaved in North America, and the abuse and trauma continued after the emancipation proclamation and after August 16, 1865, when President Andrew Johnson reversed the ruling that former slaves could receive land from former slaveholders. Even after the passing of the Thirteenth, Fourteenth, and Fifteenth amendments, the establishment of the Freedmen's Bureau, and the post–Civil War helter-skelter War Department relief efforts to establish a new social order for the nearly four million liberated former slaves, freedom was not obtained. Nearly a century and a half later, productive and fruitful living for many ALANAs is still an illusion. The quest for decency and human dignity continues to be a dream deferred. For many ALANAs, the realities of trauma and socio-race amplify their biological and emotional predispositions to distress and suffering. Science has revealed that our nervous systems are susceptible to being overwhelmed by trauma, and we now know that intrapersonal and interpersonal trauma is genetically transmitted.

Weaponizing socio-race results in trauma, and racial trauma is a darkness on the United States that creates an individual and collective shadow. Individually the shadow is the personification of aspects of the human psyche that we deny in ourselves and project onto others. Because of the fear and resentment of socio-race in America, ALANAs find it difficult to trust "Americans." They have concluded that it is not wise to trust a country and its people who treat them in hateful and destructive manners. As a therapist, I can recommend that ALANA clients protect themselves and operate freely only among known allies.

ALANAs have mastered the art of smiling and presenting a self that conceals their pain and they struggle with incentive to function as their authentic selves. The True Self is one's objective and metaphysical self. It is the self that is engulfed in the "Positive Creative Energy" of this life. However, rather than embrace the eternal good of our humanity, ALANAs often focus on the bogus self, created by our own minds, egos, and cultures. This bogus self is a pretense, a passing fad, a psychological defense constructed out of our pain and doubt. We must search for and locate the true self that is revealed in the Holy One. Rather than continue to create concepts and systems that separate and are defined by hierarchy, Americans must find the way of surrender and love. It is essential that socio-race be dismantled and reborn within God's creation not as a weapon but as a component of God's perfect diversity. Once reborn, our diversity manifests our Creator, who clothes, reveals, and transforms creation back to its incarnate redemptive form. What our world and our nation has formed around socio-race are relationships emptied of their goodness and righteousness. This trend and tendency clash with the gift of interconnectedness with the One and with one another. This human inclination set us on a path of self-destruction and disconnection.

All people—ALANAs and white Americans—must annihilate this false self that is fueled by racism and oppression. Socio-race as a harsh, violent, and divisive human condition can no longer be a tool of domination and acrimony. It is critical that we Americans shift our perspective from the smallness of tribalism and individual rights to one that recognizes our connectedness as a mosaic community created by an awesome multiplicated Creator. Only when Americans and people around the globe shift from a racist culture to a just culture will we find equity and restoration.

2

INTERSECTIONALITY

MY UNDERSTANDING OF racial trauma, equity, diversity, inclusion, and intersectionality began in childhood. One of the highlights of my life was witnessing the development of my mother as the matriarch of our family. Mom graduated from high school as the class valedictorian and fell in love with my dad after he returned home from military service. She then chose marriage and raising children over attending college. She was an amazing stay-at-home mother after her marriage to my father, and she labored tirelessly to care for her husband and seven children in Detroit, Michigan.

Life before the Detroit Revolts was challenging but very fulfilling for the McCreary family. The turmoil in the city in 1967 was an expression of feelings of no control by Black Americans and the degraded nature of their Black existence. The alienation from society and the fact that white America cherished property above people was a precursor to the urban violence of the summer of 1967.[1]

After the Detroit Revolts of 1967 and 1968 and my father's demise, my mother had to add to her previous roles of wife and mother the responsibilities of sole provider. She had to now manage the devastating effects of her husband's mental health crisis on the family and provide for the needs of her family. For years, I blamed my father for the dismantling of my family of origin and causing our descent into poverty. I revered my mother for lifting the family upon her shoulders and carrying us to safety. However, I now realize that the responsibility for our family's plight also lies with policy makers who created the structure of poverty and perpetuated the deplorable conditions of the urban cities.

For this writer, who experienced his mother doing the seemingly impossible, adolescence was a lesson in intersectionality. I did not believe then and do not believe now that people can pick themselves up by their bootstraps. However, as I have practiced and taught psychology, and pastored families in the Black church, I have watched individuals, like my mother, marshal their families, communities, and governments to support them as they lift their families out of poverty, remain in homes, and enter in and out of trauma experiences with dignity.

Intersectionality Defined

Intersectionality is a concept coined by Black feminist legal scholar Dr. Kimberlé Williams Crenshaw in 1989. In a landmark article about Black women's unique position in the United States' legal system, Dr. Crenshaw developed the analogy of traffic at an intersection to characterize how the systems of oppression literally intersect for women of color,[2] and she theorized that women of color are injured at the intersection between race discrimination and sex discrimination.

According to Crenshaw, a Black woman can possibly experience four interacting paths of discrimination: race discrimination experienced by male and female ALANAs (race); sex discrimination experienced by female ALANAs and white women (sex); the interaction of race and sex discrimination (race by sex); and an interaction of race and sex discrimination by other Black women (race by sex by Black women). According to this conceptualization, women of color are exposed to race discrimination, such as being redlined to poor neighbors with little to no resources. As a woman, she might also experience sex discrimination by a man on her job. Next, as a woman and a woman of color, she may experience discrimination of race by sex, such as being criticized for being a poor mother of color with poor children of color who behave poorly, use drugs, and are incarcerated. Lastly, Black women are vulnerable to a compounding experience of a unique Black female discrimination, by race, by sex, and by a race by sex interaction. An example of this would be criticism from other Black Americans for having light skin color and using good diction, being redlined to an under-resourced community with poor housing and subpar schools, being the recipient of unwelcomed and unprovoked sexual advances at work from the boss, and being blamed for birthing unruly children of color.

Our understanding of intersectionality has advanced since 1989. Since then, legal studies and the disciplines of sociology, women's studies, psychology, and economics have substantiated the interconnected nature of social categorizations such as race, class, and gender. We now know that the overlapping and interdependent systems of discrimination disenfranchise individuals and groups, creating deplorable conditions for ALANAs.[3]

Arguably, intersectionality is at the heart of our American immigration, nationalization, migration, segregation, integration, and upward mobility problems. The current usage of intersectionality is based upon an understanding of the interlocking systems of oppression that plague our social systems, which call attention to the complexity of trauma and race.

Another interesting idea to examine and include in our conversation about intersectionality is the caste system. Isabel Wilkerson defines a caste system as an "artificial construction, a fixed and embedded ranking of human value that sets the presumed supremacy of one group against the presumed inferiority of other groups on the basis of ancestry and often immutable traits, traits that would be neutral in the abstract but are ascribed life-and-death meaning in a hierarchy favoring the dominant caste whose forebearers designed it."[4]

American Caste System

The discussion of the caste system is important here because systemic racism has been embedded into the fabric of American society. Racism is defined as "a system of advantage and disadvantage based on social, historical, and cultural constructs of race and ethnicity."[5] A caste system is recognized by its rigidity, arbitrary boundaries used to keep the ranked groupings apart, and methods of identification designed to distinguish one caste from another and keep them in their assigned places. Racism is the tree; caste is the root system.

Throughout human history, three caste systems have stood out: the lingering, millennia-long caste system of India; the tragically accelerated, chilling, and officially vanquished caste system of Nazi Germany; and the shapeshifting, unspoken, race-based pyramid caste in the United States.

The caste system in India illuminates social stratification and inequalities outside of a clear racial hierarchy. This centuries-old caste system evolved from an understanding of local gods, goddesses, and heroes. The idea of caste is meticulously connected to Hindu beliefs, and though it is now less rigid than earlier in the country's history, caste still maintains and influences Indian society, relationships, and structures. Initially, in the Indian caste system superiority was based on conduct not on birth. Over time the hierarchy of caste developed based on power and resources as opposed to feelings or morality. That is, which groups have power, which do not, which castes are seen as worthy, and which are not. A caste system determines who gets to acquire resources and control power and who does not. Caste is about respect, authority, and assumptions of competence—who is accorded these and who is not.

Germany established its caste system after losing World War I and blaming the loss on its Jewish population. Jews were dehumanized as the out-group, stigmatized, and blamed for the economic difficulties experienced by the country after the war. Because of this caste process six million Jews and five million others were murdered during the twelve-year rule of the Third Reich.

In the American caste system, the primary indicator of rank is race. The social construct of race divides humans in the United States based on appearance. Race in America ascribes value to or does not ascribe value to entire human groups and our unique race-caste system affects Americans beyond our conscious awareness. Race and caste are embedded into the core of our unconscious minds based on human characteristics, ranking and ruling expectations, stereotypes, behavior, and relationships. Caste and race are neither synonymous nor mutually exclusive. They can and do coexist in the same culture and serve to reinforce each other. Wilkerson explains this synchronicity by stating that race in the United States serves as the visible agent and unseen force of caste. She describes caste as the bones and race as the skin of the American caste system.

This writer can recall having experienced the synchronicity of race and caste as a college professor in the southeast region of the United States. One such experience occurred when my wife and I were looking to purchase a home in Richmond, Virginia, near the university where I was serving as a professor. A white colleague's wife "took a liking" to our family and wanted our daughter to live in a neighborhood with a great public school system, which turned out to be a predominantly white neighborhood in which very few people of color could purchase homes. Our realtor found a house in the west-end of Richmond. We moved in, were welcomed by neighbors, and flourished in that home. However, when mowing my lawn, I was often asked by passing white people how much I charged for my services. We also enrolled our precocious five-year-old daughter in a nearby Montessori school, and I had the joy of taking her to school and my wife picked her up. One morning my daughter and I wanted to avoid the carpool, so we parked in the adjacent parking lot and raced through a wooded pathway that led from the parking lot to the school. We had a wonderful time laughing and of course my daughter won the race to class. Later that morning when I arrived at my office on campus, my dean called me in and asked me to call my daughter's school. The school told me that a driver on River Road had reported that a Black man was chasing a child on the property, trying to kidnap or harm her. The police had also shown up at the school and were investigating to see if I was the child's father.

Another race and caste incident occurred when my daughter and I were walking together on Monument Avenue in Richmond, Virginia, during the period of the Golden Age Killer. We had just driven from church, dressed in our church clothing, had parked, and walked to my colleague's home on Monument Avenue for a faculty gathering. While we were there enjoying the affair, the police arrived and asked me to step outside. I did as requested and so did my colleagues. The policeman reported that he had been called to investigate a report that a Black man fitting my description was walking up and down the street checking doors, and they feared I was the Golden Age Killer. Before I could respond, my faculty colleagues informed the officer that I had been with them and could not have done what I was being accused of doing.

In these instances, my race and out-of-caste position and social status confronted the powerful infrastructure of race and caste and created an intersection and interaction effect that affects how I govern and how I approach my external world. This is a reality that ALANAs live with in the United States. ALANAs are always aware of our assigned position, place, and status. We realize that, to many Americans, no matter how accomplished and refined we think we are, there are those who view us as an N-Word with a PhD. And even though we have developed tools for coping with living as ALANAs and have been socialized by our family and family systems to be prepared for these types of interactions, they still affect us.

Sociologist Patricia Hill Collins describes intersectionality as a matrix of domination.[6] She suggests that a dynamic system of inter-locked oppressions, societally formed and organized, have produced and sustained inequality among ALANAS. Collins expands our under-standing of intersectionality by focusing our attention on the interac-tion of unequal social systems. She suggests that these unequal systems shape the lives of multiple marginalized people in North America and around the world.

Assuming an intersecting, interacting, and interlocking approach to the analysis of race and trauma, this book explores the manners in which intersectionality of race, class, and gender complicate trauma for all Americans, particularly ALANAs. The analyses are contained here unapologetically. This book is written for those who care about the wellbeing of ALANAs and those in need of healing, including all people seeking to grow through traumatic experiences.

As mentioned previously, the construct of race refers to social groups partially and inconsistently defined by differences in observable physical characteristics such as skin color and hair. Yet, race also signifies ethnic, cultural, linguistic, and religious differences that animate persistent conflict between social groups.[7] Thus, classism is a variable which is critical to analyses of race and trauma. The discipline of psychology typically considers the individual to be the primary focus of analysis and historically has secondarily investigated the effect of class on mental wellbeing and race. Classism is included in our discussion of intersectionality because classism is manifested in society through the practices, attitudes, assumptions, behaviors, and policies through which social institutions function to perpetuate the deprivation and low status of poor people.[8] Classism interacts with other forms of oppression to contribute to the interlocking systems of oppression for ALANAs and it has been correlated with high levels of unemployment and unresolved grief. Unemployment and unresolved grief often lead to unhealthy feelings of being cheated and hurt, an inability to gain closure, a fear of facing the past, the maintenance of family secrets, and an inability to disclose and communicate openly. Classism perpetuates a state of poverty, and poverty is typically a by-product of a lack—of good jobs, of good education, of food and clothing, of good infrastructure— and the result of social injustice and little governmental support. Factor in race and you have a clear example of intersectionality.

Gender is considered a category, most often "male" or "female," assigned by doctors at birth based on a baby's genitalia and chromosomes. Broadly defined, it denotes a range of identities that do not correspond to established ideas of male and female, and it focuses on the social and legal status of identities rather than biological ones. It is a set of expectations from society about behaviors, characteristics, and thoughts. Recently, there has been a great deal of disagreement surrounding the issue of broadening the discussion about sex and gender, particularly around the notion that one's gender identity is socially defined and internally perceived. The belief that a person's labeling of the self can be based on how much they align or do not align with what they understand their options for gender to be is hotly contested in some circles. Our understanding of gender discrimination has also been broadened by feminist and womanist scholars. It is widely accepted that there are four aspects to gender discrimination: (i) ideological: gender rankings, valuing, and beliefs; (ii) institutional: systems, laws, media, and structures; (iii) interpersonal: biases within people's attitudes, interactions, and actions; and (iv) intrapersonal/internalized: individual conscious and unconscious, beliefs, ideas, feelings, and behaviors.

Many of my conservative colleagues bristle at the differentiation, separation, and expansion of the concept of gender and sex. This writer prefers to engage different thinkers in conversations, hoping to breathe life and awareness into the conversation. At times, as a cis-gendered, heterosexual, upper-middle-class, Black American male, these conversations entail intellectual and emotional voyages into unchartered territory. Thus, we value and use broad inclusive language in this book mainly because we respect the voices and self-definition of all people. We will resist assuming a hierarchical position of demanding and defining person terms according to this writer's limited understanding and write in a manner that seeks to engage and encourage fruitful conversation. In this book, the term "sexism/genderism" will be used.

The term and concept of intersectionality has become an offensive and rejected topic for conversative thinkers and a political hot button for many others. Yet, intersectionality remains a reasonable explanation for the social stagnation of ALANAs. When we consider the intersectionality of race and gender, we can more readily identify the manifestation and prolongation of trauma and race in this country (see Figure 2.2).

In promoting a conversation on race and trauma, this writer views those who reject a cogent discussion of the complexities that surround race and trauma as polarizing and finger pointing. Some people seek to live guided by the ego-self or false self and are history-stoppers. They use politics and rhetoric to defend their own status and the status quo of the world that sustains them. They are fearful people who think that whatever way the wind blows it will blow on them and their agenda. These self-centered hierarchical oppressors have no desire to change and move beyond their small agendas.

This writer is calling for courage from those who are inspired to labor with the wounds of racial trauma. Courage to have faith, love, and hope in being better human beings; courage to trust our own experience and accept the experiences of others without criticism

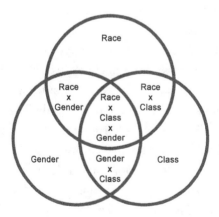

Figure 2.2. Venn diagram of intersectionality of race, class, and gender.

and judgment. This book is calling for a new transformational system. One in which trusting and believing triumphs over our tendency to be self-centered. This is a clarion call for human healers to further develop their gifts, insights, and techniques to change the self and others.

One of the more helpful tools of a healer is to recognize the defense mechanisms being used by those against or in favor of an action. In this case, valuing the use of intersectionality and valuing an individual's rights to self-define is an important aspect of the healing process around trauma and race. Critics of the construct of intersectionality base their criticism on a belief that intersectionality was birthed out of identity politics. They argue that it villainizes white males and puts forth the perspective that the more victim identities a person possesses, the closer that individual is to winning the most victimized person or group award. Of course, those who seek division will see division and those who promote rejection will find concepts and constructs to reject.

The inclusion of intersectionality around this discussion on race and trauma is not proposed to cause anyone to feel guilty. Rather, this is a call for healers to consider the complexities of the human psyche and human experience and to mobilize every resource to address the complexity of race and trauma. Even the most challenging experiences can end up being good in one way or another if we don't shut down and close them off. Take for example the repugnant Tuskegee Syphilis Study, conducted from the 1930s to the 1970s with 399 Black men. A total of 201 Black men were enrolled in the study as control subjects and were never told the true nature of the study. Twenty-eight Black men in the study died of syphilis when there was a cure; one hundred additional Black men in the study died from syphilis-related complications when there was an available cure; at least forty Black wives of men in the study were infected; and nineteen Black children of these men contracted syphilis at birth when there was a cure for syphilis.

The Tuskegee Syphilis Study itself is not significant to our discussion on race and trauma, but the study became the catalyst that brought about reforms in the atrocious way human beings were treated in scientific experiments, resulting in the Belmont Report of 1978. As a direct result of the abuses and unethical practices of the Tuskegee Syphilis Study, the Belmont Report established what is now called the Ethical Principles and Guidelines for the Protection of Human Subjects. The report remains the primary foundation for specific policies that currently govern research on humans. The three key principles of the Belmont Report are respect of person (informed consent), beneficence (benefit or help), and risk versus benefits (do no harm), and these are taught to every scientist and practiced worldwide by scientist-practitioners.

Humans tend to guard against threats of change by applying one of the common psychological defenses. Dr. Anna Freud and others have offered nine frequently used psychological defenses:[9] denial (refusing to accept reality); repression (pushing anxiety out of consciousness); projection (attributing unwanted emotions and thoughts to another); displacement (redirecting impulses to a less threatening target); regression (reverting to an earlier stage of development); sublimation (displacing unacceptable emotion into acceptable behaviors); rationalization (cognitive distortion of the facts); reaction formation (behaving in a manner opposite of thoughts or feelings); and identification with the enemy or aggressor (victim adopts the behaviors of the victimizer).

It is helpful to attribute characteristics of defensiveness to groups that politically and socially opposed highlighting the effects of racism on ALANAs rather than attribute it to evil. To defend against intersectionality by denying its existence and questioning its motives and credibility, which is what frequently occurs, is classic human psychological mechanisms at work. Nevertheless, the existence of defensive opposing political and theoretical positions to intersectionality does not negate the reality of the interlocking influence of race, gender, and class on the race-based stressful experiences of ALANAs. The intersection of racism, casteism, sexism/genderism, and classism allows a more comprehensive assessment and evaluation of their impact on race and trauma.

Racism/casteism, sexism/genderism, and classism in the United States are national problems, and understanding the intersectionality between them allows us to comprehend the phenomena of racial trauma and other race-based stress more clearly.[10] Understanding the complexity of variables affecting trauma and race, such as racial stress, race-based stress, or racial trauma, enhances our abilities to treat, diagnose, repair, and heal racial trauma. Furthermore, because of the seemingly permanent presence of race-based stressors, investigating the complexities or intersectionality of traumatic race injuries is important in treating PTSD. A clearer understanding of race-based stressors (race, gender, and class) will inform and enhance the treatment of racial trauma.

Accepting that sociopolitical context plays a significant role in any analysis of trauma and race is imperative. For example, lynching is a sociopolitical form of racial trauma. Initially, lynching was a form of punishment for criminal behavior in Europe and America. But over the years, in America, lynching morphed into terrorist acts against Black Americans far beyond punishment for criminal behavior. Today, lynching is a trigger of historical trauma for Black Americans. For Black Americans it is like the Holocaust for Jewish Americans and the internment camps for Japanese Americans. Lynching thus can activate a fight, flight, or freeze response in African Americans. Healers treating them benefit from the knowledge that even if the client is not afraid of being lynched, they will become aware of and alert to the impending sociopolitical danger. It is a mistake to ignore the impact of years of enslavement, deportations, forced migrations, and ostracizations on the psycho-social-spiritual wellbeing of ALANAs. Intersectionality offers an investigative and interpretative conceptualization explanation for the existence and treatment of racial trauma. The problems surrounding the intersectionality of race, gender, and class in relation to racial trauma are local and global.

Intersectionality is experienced by people of color throughout the world. I went to Haiti as a pastoral psychologist to work with pastors and their families a week after Haiti experienced a 7.0 magnitude earthquake in January 2010. I will never forget arriving on the runway of Toussaint Louverture International Airport in Port-au-Prince. The damage to the airport was so extensive that we had to exit the plane on the runway and walk from the plane to the terminal. Upon leaving the airport and arriving in the city, seeing the damage to buildings, the loss of lives, and the homelessness was harrowing. The Haitian people, who had lost everything but their lives, created homes and shelters from scraps of tin, discarded construction materials, tarps, and blankets and these areas became known as tent cities. Haitian women and children in particular reported suffering abuse and hardships in those communities.

The mission organization that sent me to Haiti took me and three hundred Haitians to a mountain retreat facility for two weeks of worship, Bible study, and workshops to facilitate emotional and spiritual healing. I had transported my computer, LCD projector, and speakers with me, anticipating using my technology to engage and entertain the participants. It turned out that there was no electricity, so I combined Bible study with role-plays and group activities. I was excited about the work. I did a Bible study on Daniel and the lion's den in which a pastor played Daniel and laid in the middle of hungry angry lions. The lions were played by children, who circled him, growling and snapping their teeth at him. I then directed the mothers to surround the lions in prayer and fathers to surround the mothers praying and watching. I thought this Bible study was insightful and informative. We discussed the dangers of individualism and the power of community. The activity demonstrated to them how one strong man could not easily pick up Daniel and carry him out of the lion's den, but that seven people, each lifting a part of Daniel, could collectively carry him out of danger.

In the group activities and role-plays, we focused on the trauma that had arisen in the community because of the earthquake. I was targeting the trauma resulting from the serious injuries, loss of property, and loss of lives. The people performed the role-plays dramatically well. Women dressed in costume, characterizing their unspeakable distress as they acted out searching for their lost children among the rubble. The young people acted out the drugs and gang problems in Haiti, as well as the mental health challenges of depression and suicidal ideation they were experiencing.

When the role-plays ended, I asked everyone there to circle around the actors, and I began to sing the hymn "Amazing Grace" in English. Before long a very powerful and active woman, who I called the "Queen Mother," joined in singing the song with me in Haitian Creole. Moments later, the entire group began singing and the actors in the middle began to cry and wail. It was a powerful cathartic healing moment for the entire community.

The young people performed role-plays to express their pain and agonies. They used belts as nooses and pencils as needles to illustrate their pain. After their role-plays, I was deeply moved, and I joined them on the floor and through the interpreter said that I was doing what Jesus did, leaving the found and going after the lost sheep. I was taking their pain as my pain. I was offering my life for their lives. I was asking them to journey with me to a universal love, a divine love, that could heal all wounds. At this the "Queen Mother" joined me and others left their seats and began hugging the young people. This was another powerful cathartic healing moment for the youth and the community.

I knew we were getting to the heart of their pain and despair. I knew we were doing critical and essential trauma and race work. Suddenly, the double doors to the room we were in opened and in marched a group of ten to twelve local male pastors. I had seen them leave earlier and I was delighted to see them return. I was blessed by their presence and impressed by their military-like style. They reminded me of how the brothers from the Fruit of Islam marched in places and spaces to protect the vulnerable during my adolescence in Detroit. But then I noticed the faces of the participants and knew something was awry. The pastors marched in and lined up side-by-side across the back of the room and stopped abruptly, glared at me intensely, and then turned their backs to me and stood there. I asked my interpreter what this gesture meant. He told me that the pastors were shunning me and my teaching. They were saying that Haiti did not need what I was offering. They did not agree that I should have the people gathered there, particularly the women and young people, reflecting on their pain. They believed my teaching was humiliating and degrading, and they wanted me to limit my interventions to preaching and praying only.

As the interpreter and I were speaking to the pastors, I noticed the "Queen Mother" of the group had discreetly pulled out a cell phone and was having an intense quiet conversation with someone. Five minutes later a tall proud man walked through the door. He called the pastors to him for conference. I asked the interpreter who this man was and was told he was the superintendent and husband of the "Queen Mother." After he spoke to the pastors they returned to their seats and participated in the remainder of the workshop. The superintendent pulled me aside, apologized for the misunderstanding, and thanked me for my work. He said his wife had told him of what we had been doing and she shared that they needed to emote and get the pain of the tragedies out into the open.

Intersectionality of race, class, and gender is one thing and the complexities surrounding trauma and race is another thing. The pastors were ignoring both the intersectionality of race, class, and gender and the complexities of trauma and race. The history of Haiti is filled with racial trauma. The sociopolitical climate in Haiti is replete with gender and class oppression. I was operating in ignorance of the race issue that was created by my presence as a Black American at a Christian retreat after the worst earthquake in Haiti's history.

The pastors who reacted to my teaching most likely initially felt their reactions were biblical and had nothing to do with a trauma response. However, they were really being affected by the presence of intrusive trauma symptoms being acted out by the workshop participants. Like many people who experience trauma, or treat those who do, the pastors did not realize that the correlation between the images, thoughts, recollections, and nightmares being reexperienced by all were reminders of the stressful events of the earthquake and representative of the stressful life events of Haitian citizenship prior to the earthquake. The pastors were exhibiting avoidance symptoms. They were not being disrespectful, they were attempting to avoid symbols of their trauma. They were attempting to control both their own emotions and the emotions of the women, youth, and children. As with most trauma situations, it was the arousal symptoms that received the most attention. The role-plays of the women and the young people expressed their hypervigilance, startled responses, irritability, and angry outbursts, which overwhelmed the pastors and led to their exit from the room.

The Haitians are a proud people of African descent, governed by people of African descent. They are also a people who have been afflicted by political corruption, international isolation, internal and external economic abuse, and a multitude of other social impediments. Tragedy was not new to the pastors and their reactions to my interventions were not unusual. They were being the protectors ascribed by their roles as male pastors.

It was clear to me that I was dealing with a trauma response. Many would think that my being Black American would be an advantage, but my Blackness and my being sent from a Black American mission agency complicated the emotionality in the space. Yes, my presence provided a familiarity that created a therapeutic relationship. But my presence also served to create a therapeutic environment that intensified their race stressors and pressed us forward for a cathartic confrontation. My nationality and race status triggered a complicated emotional response. If I had not understood the deeper context of their reaction, the confrontation could have been disastrous. It would have been easy to feel personally attacked by the pastors. I could have reacted defensively to their intervention. But, to work as a pastoral psychologist for transformation requires transparency and patience. Rather than approaching the confrontation defensively, I assumed a liberation, Afrocentric, and family system orientation of observing, learning, and engaging. I was more interested in being humble, present, and transparent with the group than being the expert in charge.[11] I had nothing to prove. I was there for the Haitian people. I was there to help them heal from the devastation of the earthquake. My task was to partner with them in their recovery and to serve as a pastoral psychologist for them through their inherently complex trauma experiences.

The Bible studies, sermons, and role-plays the Haitian families participated in were the catalyst that resulted in the cathartic experiences and prompted the intersectionality of female and male leaderships. The "Queen Mother" and the superintendent in the Haiti example point to the importance of mutual female and male leadership. I know my interventions at that retreat would have been less effective were it not for the advocacy and participation of the "Queen Mother." Also, it would have been difficult, if not impossible, to have negotiated the demands of the pastors without the creditability and influence of the superintendent. Furthermore, if the superintendent had not listened to the counsel of his wife and come into the workshop, the effectiveness of my interventions with the group would have most likely been negated. While the interventions were clearly helpful to the group, the importance of the support and participation from the community, the "Queen Mother," and the superintendent must be noted.

Ofttimes, we traumatize our clients and parishioners with a sexist conceptualization of gender. We function in practice and in ministry without reconciling the tension of living under the curse or being free to live under the new covenant. We resist entering counseling with a true collaborative equalitarian reciprocal leadership style. Often our need for male power and authority hinders the effectiveness of our interventions. I recall discussing leadership with my life-partner shortly after our marriage. In ignorance, I told her that since I was the one already licensed into ministry, she needed to be my helpmeet and support my ministry. I had not yet learned that "helpmeet" in the Hebrew is *Ezer k'gnedo*, which means to give "help that opposes." My early sexist miseducation had been drilled into me during my adolescence by the teaching of the church I attended. Fortunately, my family socialization made me amenable to the feminist and womanist teachings that I was introduced to during my later seminary education, and these teachings corrected my misconceptions.

There is a movement in some churches now that promotes complementarianism over and against equalitarianism. Complementarians assume a literal interpretation of the King James translation of Christian Scripture. Complementarianism affirms that only men should hold church leadership positions over men, and takes a patriarchal view of the family, the view that a man should love his wife as Christ loved the church, and a woman should submit to her husband as the church submits to Christ. An equalitarian perspective focuses on men and women both holding church leadership positions, spouses having equal responsibility for family, marriage as a partnership of two equals submitting to one another, and the roles in the union being ability-based and not gender-based. The intent of this book is to promote the intersectionality and interactions between the two positions rather than promoting one position over the other. Leadership is very important, regardless of the race, class, or gender of the leader. I am suggesting that healers will be more effective if they are attentive to the intersection of race, class, and gender. What is necessary is a fair and balanced treatment of the issues of race, class, and gender, coupled with an awareness of the complexities they bring to race and trauma efforts. Fair treatment in relation to the roles of women and men in society and in the church is not as simple as making edicts and proclamations, one way or the other. What is required is an intersectional perspective that examines the interactions of constructs such as gender, race, class, and trauma in an intelligent investigative way.

I have witnessed and consulted with many families and communities that are impoverished and trapped in ineffective living situations because they failed to attend to the inherent complexities of trauma. I recall consulting with a family in crisis years ago that did not comprehend the complexities of their situation. They did not see how their careers, their failed attempts at conceiving children, their diverse spiritual and religious traditions, and their childhood traumas were individually and collectively affecting their marriage. The families and I spent time unpacking each individual experience and examining the collective and intersectional impact of their life experiences on their relationship, and fortunately healing occurred and their homes and marriages became more satisfying for them.

When an individual or group is confronted with the threat of death, serious injury, or some other threat to physical integrity, then traumatic emotional injuries can occur. Long-term stressors resulting from jobs, children, poverty, maturity, and developmental delays can produce unpredictable emotions, mood swings, flashbacks, strained relationships, and even physical symptoms like headaches or nausea. When we add racial, sexual, and class traumas, such as those that descend from former enslaved people, like the fear of deportation, sexual exploitation, poor resources, and redlined communities, trauma is further complicated. This does not make one community's trauma more significant than another's, but it does indicate that a different approach might be effective.

Dr. Crenshaw argued for a strong consideration of a collective feminist and antiracist therapeutic approach with ALANA consumers, as opposed to an individualist approach. The individual is important, but the individual is only a portion of the whole. The "I," or *ego* in Latin, is described in Freudian psychiatry as the part of us that arbitrates and mediates the conflict between the "id" (immature childish self) and the "super-ego" (the parental consciousness of the self). Thus, the ego is a part of an interlocking personality system. To remove any part of the personality system from the personality would only serve to undermine the effectiveness of the whole system and produce additional pathology. The individual, therefore, must not be the reference point for lasting substantial change. The all-important individual is a part of the all-important individual's system.

Spirituality has always been a part of my coping and personality system. However, as a graduate student working on my doctorate in psychology, I found that many of my colleagues perceived my spiritual principles as having no place in psychology. This resulted in the development of my personal lifegiving mantra: my soul is not for sale. I now intersperse spiritual principles with psychological principles throughout my work and throughout this book. Over the years, I have had the honor to shepherd loved ones, members of the community, families, and enemies through their trauma. Trauma is a powerful life experience that uniquely positions an individual or group to lose selfishness and rise above tribalism. Many people in mainstream clinical practice will find themselves uncomfortable with spiritual language. But intersectional thinking allows us to bring to the healing space tools from other disciplines, including spirituality, to move over the inadequate small self and allow the adequate real self to emerge; a self that leads us beyond the blind narrow-mindedness of "I" to an enlightenment and availability that empowers the "us" to overcome life's limitations.

Intersectionality pulls together socialization, consciousness, and culturalization to facilitate an examination of the false self that allows the false self to move aside. Trauma grants access to the raw material of the soul through which we can help groups and individuals find peace and harmony in their pain. Traumatic experiences focus us on what is important and create learning opportunities like few other life experiences, and traumatic situations force us to examine our relationships and improve or eliminate boundaries, chasms, and schisms.

The language of the soul is discussed in psychology and spirituality. Soul work is not only about salvation and being holy. Soul work is about stripping away illusions, letting go of pretense, and breaking open our understanding and our hearts. In the language of the Christian Church, trauma can be a calvary experience, a death, dying, resurrection, and ascension encounter.

3

BENIGN NEGLECT

I WAS FORTUNATE to engage in soul work during my psychology education. In the late 1980s I had the honor of training as a graduate psychology student with Dr. John G. (Jack) Corazzini. Jack was director of the university counseling center, a group therapy professor, and the clinical supervisor at the university. He was a no-nonsense, psychodynamic-oriented therapist and a former Catholic priest who pulled no punches and did not tolerate foolishness. At the time of my training, Jack was in his early fifties and very proud of his Italian Catholic heritage. I will never forget the time Jack stated, "It is not what you do that is important, it's what you do with what has been done."[1]

In our group therapy class Jack used Irvin Yalom's *Theory and Practice of Group Psychotherapy* and Paulo Freire's *Pedagogy of the Oppressed* as our textbooks.[2] I had read *Pedagogy of the Oppressed* in seminary and was pumped to finally demonstrate my understanding of oppression and the oppressed. I was determined to share my knowledge and insight as a seminary graduate from a historically Black seminary and a young man from inner-city Detroit, Michigan.

Freire had given me a language to critically understand my anger toward systems of oppression, injustice, and poverty, as well as my frustration with the vicissitudes of life. I had finally reconciled my admiration for Rev. Dr. Martin Luther King Jr. with my love for el-Hajj Malik el-Shabazz (Malcolm X). I had made peace with my male privilege, tamed my antipathy toward hierarchies, and learned to value being an ally to women. I tempered my disdain of organized religion with my love of God and abiding spirituality. On an intuitive level, I felt empowered to have a serious conversation with this powerful white man who so effectively used my favorite book about education and oppression in a group therapy course.

Counseling with ALANAs

One day in class, Dr. Corazzini was talking about manipulation in counseling relationships. He suggested that every client used manipulation in their interactions with the counselor, and every counselor used manipulation to facilitate successful therapy.

I was overwhelmed by the urge to speak out. This radical reconstitution of counseling appalled me. I understood Freire's discussion of manipulation as a tool used by oppressors and an oppressive system; manipulation was a pitfall and a consequence of domination and domestication. What I did not see was the application of manipulation in counseling. Dr. Corazzini appeared to be manipulating the class, recolonizing me, and mocking Freire. Bubbling with rage and indignation, I used my voice as power to stand against this perceived oppression.

Going against my personal desire to be seen as competent, I took the personal risk of appearing incompetent by strongly stating an objection. "Jack," I said, "you are incorrect. Counseling is about helping; it is not about manipulating the client. I don't know Yalom, but I know Freire, and his book does not promote manipulation." Jack looked at me kindly and said, "Micah, you are manipulating me now. How is your manipulation good and mine bad? What makes your manipulation acceptable and mine reprehensible?"

Whether Jack was manipulating the class or I manipulating Jack are irreverent questions. What was important was that Jack raised issues and questions that were thought-provoking. I reacted according to my anger and my trauma. What was Jack's response? Jack "held" my anger and my trauma. I felt heard, challenged, and cared for. More importantly, I felt our disagreement while simultaneously feeling valued. Jack was not mocking me or justifying his position as an elite oppressor.

This exchange was powerful because Jack was a white man and most of my childhood rage and trauma revolves around white men. When the National Guard was called to Detroit during the Detroit Revolts, it was a white national guardsman who opened the hatch of the tank and glared at me. It was a white man who was driving drunk and hit me with his car, landing me in the hospital. The driver befriended me until my mother decided not to press charges against him; I never saw him again. It was white counselors at my summer fellowship who told me to build the I-beam rather than undertaking the more demanding computer programming and coding tasks, and it was a white counselor at my engineering college who told me I was not well-prepared enough to study engineering.

My feelings may have been unfair, but in all honesty, I did not trust or value white men. My posture toward them was anger. I now understand that my trauma centered around men, Black and white, and their role in my development. My training with Jack helped me not only recognize my trauma but also develop my power, my style, and my approach to therapy. Because Jack embraced my anger and my rage toward white men and toward myself, I learned to stay in the therapeutic space with my clients, using transference and counter-transference to heal us both.

I now realize that it was rare, then, for an American in the dominant caste to act out of caste and welcome me as human. In the true tradition of Paulo Freire, Jack Corazzini encouraged ingenuity and dialogue as the epistemology of the therapeutic relationship. Jack promoted authentic dialogue in counseling as a way of knowing. He dismantled centuries of caste-constructed walls between us and became an ally in my war against dissention and dehumanization. I am forever grateful for his teaching this lesson while being the object of the lesson.

For most mental health professionals trained in the decades preceding the 1990s, training was eccentric. We were trained from a variety of therapy orientations. For example, my graduate school cohort was exposed to group therapy, client-centered psychotherapy, gestalt psychotherapy, cognitive behavioral therapy, and family therapy. Cultural therapy training also became available through the Association of Black Psychologists and the Asian American Psychological Association. As a result, I developed a theoretical orientation that combined client-centered, cultural (spiritual), and family systems therapies. I later added dialectical behavior therapy (DBT) to my repertoire to enhance my work with trauma, addiction, and abuse clientele. Engaging in clinical practice with individuals, families, and communities struggling to overcome life challenges is a high honor. Following in the tradition of Jack Corazzini, Nancy Boyd-Franklin, and Carl Whitaker, I came to deeply value the role of counselor as a critical component of change.

In counseling, clients often begin the relationship with discomfort. They are entering this new artificial relationship with suspicion. As someone devoted and dedicated to the healing arts of counseling, I conceptualize counseling as a work of the heart. Therefore, I had to make authentic, deep connections with my clients. After establishing the therapeutic relationship, I would then move to resolve the presenting problem. I also found it important to serve as an antagonist with my clients to actively oppose their maladaptive behaviors—to force them to confront their issues. My counseling mission was "To labor with committed families and individuals to foster health, healing, and wholeness." For me, psychotherapy was not a stigmatizing endeavor, but a proven healing tool that did not work like a medical pill, but rather worked through the counselor–client relationship.[3]

In the tradition of my mentors, I felt called to wed academics and church to clinical practice. Thus, when I accepted the faculty position at the university where I earned my doctorate degree, I asked to teach the multicultural counseling class to first-year counseling psychology PhD students. I also developed a small private practice alongside my work as a tenure-track faculty member. Additionally, my wife and I began working very part-time at our church as parish teachers. These moves were made to keep me, the PhD, grounded, connected, and accessible to the communities I loved so deeply.

My deep love for clients propelled me to work as a pastoral psychologist with trauma and race. My practice was built on the understanding of four critical counseling components: therapeutic relationship and alliance, agreement on counseling task, mutual acceptance of the presenting problem, and agreement on processes and procedures. Even when these components are established, every practitioner must come to the realization that there are client idiosyncrasies and extra-therapeutic factors that influence counseling; some things are beyond the counselor's control. Factors such as personal motivation, social support network, and life events influence therapy outcomes. These factors can be discussed in treatment, but only the client has the power to alter them.

Even so, we now know from psychotherapy outcome studies that one of the most significant producers of positive counseling outcomes is the therapeutic relationship between the therapist and the client.[4] The counselor and client must mutually agree on the counseling tasks and the counseling goals, and the counselor must facilitate a positive alliance with the client. The counselor must present a cogent rationale for the work they will require the client to do. The counselor must offer an adequate explanation and rationale for the presenting problems, and they must implement a process and a set of procedures consistent with the rationale to advance their work and alleviate the presenting problems.

I still recall a session with a young African American male who was failing in school, bullying others, and being bullied at home. We started counseling because his school required it for him to remain enrolled. This young man had been involved in several physical altercations at school. However, it was unclear whether he was an instigator or a recipient of the fight. Recognized as bright and talented in science, he walked with a chip on his shoulder. Initially, our counseling resembled the opening session between the counselor and client in the movie *Good Will Hunting*. After several unproductive sessions, I said, "Young man, I do not believe you want to grow. So, I need to end our session a few minutes early to get to my martial arts class." His demeanor changed and he asked if I was a serious practitioner. I shared that I did have a black belt and enjoyed helping my teacher teach. He then asked if I could teach him. I said, "Yes, if you will commit to counseling for eight weeks. After eight weeks we would reassess your situation and you and I will decide whether martial arts, counseling, or both are best for your growth and development. What do you think?" He agreed.

What I have just described is an interpersonal-oriented counseling or psychotherapeutic process. Accordingly, I use presence and interpersonal counseling techniques to create a therapeutic environment and a holding space for the client to heal. This approach is also a systemic family systems approach, in which I served as the protagonist and disrupted his typical pattern and system. I was attempting to use my presence in his life to disrupt his equilibrium and alter his behavioral patterns. This was also an attempt to create a new reality or culture by using the techniques of transference and countertransference, negotiating boundaries, attending to the client, building the relationship, and addressing attachment issues.

Some counselors see this interpersonal approach as "wonky" and unnecessary, but my experience has taught me that if the client does not engage in the process, counseling usually does not work. Counseling is interpersonal and intrapersonal. It does not mean the counselor has to manipulate the client to like the counselor. But, as taught by Jack Corazzini, the counselor must manipulate the situation to be amenable to therapeutic work. The counselor must use counseling skills or psychotherapy techniques to create therapeutic and artificial relationships—to negotiate a space where clients are willing to participate in the process of having their interpersonal functioning altered. This type of relationship-based treatment seeks to develop and maintain a trusting and secure counselor–client relationship. Using counseling skills in this manner focuses on empowering the client to cultivate personal safety, relational stability, the skills to alleviate problematic behaviors, and trauma resolution strategies.

Some counselors have asked me, in supervision and in consultation, what to do when they are not a martial artist. I share that with adolescents I have played pool, taken walks to libraries and bookstores, and conducted counseling over a mancala stone game.[5] With adults I have used mandalas, coffee breaks, gestalt empty-chair techniques, and bibliotherapy. A few other activities, such as Rubik's Cubes, adult coloring books, chess, and checkers, could also be used. The issue is for the counselor to connect and develop trust. Because of our cultural shift to an information, media, and internet society, the counselor may not be as effective in counseling if they simply reflect the emotions and words of the client. More creative joining measures and techniques are necessary in today's counseling environment.

No matter the setting or method, the counselor must take control of the counselor's effectiveness. A counselor can master behavioral, intuitive, and cognitive strategies that resolve relationship questions in the client before they are even asked. As the counselor masters the skills of assessing and integrating verbal and nonverbal client feedback into the counseling session and therapeutic relationship, better counseling outcomes are achieved.[6]

Much like what Dr. Corazzini did with me, the counselor can develop a counselor alliance with the client. The counselor can consciously practice and apply relationship-enhancing techniques, such as meta-communications in counseling, to set a foundation for effective therapy. Meta-communication skills are the indirect cues—tone of voice, gestures, body language, and so forth—that counselors can use to communicate to and interpret messages from the client regarding the counseling relationship.[7] With ALANA clients meta-communication can be used to assess and ascertain information about socio-racial, gender, and cultural factors that can be used to strengthen the counseling relationship.

After many years as a practicing pastoral psychologist, it is comforting to learn, from outcome research studies and the progress of my clients, that what we do as counselors in therapy has been found to be effective in resolving emotional and systemic difficulties for clients. It is reassuring to ascertain that there is little variation in counseling effectiveness based on the type of therapy or model of therapy used. As a counseling supervisor, it is rewarding to discover that the therapeutic alliance and therapist skills of counselors, regardless of the orientation and techniques used, are critical counseling phenomena.

In addition to interpersonal counseling factors, there is another critical component to working with traumatized clients, which is broadly named empirical laboratory-based intervention or evidence-based treatment. Classic evidence-based treatments have been developed, tested, and proven very effective with many mental health challenges. Evidence-based principles and methodologies provide excellent resources for mental health professionals to help clients develop the skills necessary to navigate the world outside of counseling,[8] and evidence-based interventions have helped thousands of people who otherwise would have suffered more and longer. Evidence-based programs integrate the best available research with clinical expertise in the context of patient characteristics, culture, and preference.

I experienced this firsthand when I began working as a substance abuse therapist with clients suffering from drug addiction and personality disorders. Dialectical behavior therapy (DBT) is a proven evidence-based treatment approach. I studied and was certified as a DBT therapist and then incorporated the methods and procedures into the treatment, combining DBT components of dialectics, mindfulness, wise mind, distress tolerance, problem solving, emotional regulation, and interpersonal effectiveness training with my "standard" interpersonal psychotherapy, family systems therapy, and motivational interviewing. The result was a dynamic recovery program.

As stated earlier, it is necessary to treat trauma and complex trauma with training in interpersonal–relational-focused mental health counseling and competence with an evidence-based intervention program. This balance allows the counselor to develop a healing space by creating a therapeutic alliance, helping the client trust the counseling process, and providing the skills essential for the client to navigate their challenges outside of the counseling setting.

Trauma and Complex Trauma

Four therapeutic factors have been proven to lead to the best therapy outcomes: understanding the client and extra-therapeutic factors; developing good therapist techniques; strong therapeutic relationship factors; and the use of effective models and counseling programs. Moreover, clinical work with clients experiencing PTSD, anxiety, depression, racism, sexual abuse, drug addiction, sexism, and identity issues requires additional alertness and clinical sophistication more easily obtained when a counselor combines all four therapeutic factors.

A trauma is a stress-based challenge, and working with trauma patients who have experienced a strong emotional response to a terrible event like an accident, rape, or natural disaster requires the counselor to be a master of the four therapeutic factors above. Traumatic stressors are defined in the *Diagnostic and Statistical Manual of Mental Disorders* (DSM-5) as follows:

> *a direct personal experience of an event that involves actual or threatened death or serious injury, or other threat to one's physical integrity; witnessing an event that involves death, injury, or a threat to the physical integrity of another person; learning about unexpected or violent death, serious harm, or threat of death or injury experienced by a family member or other close associate others.*[9]

In recent decades, there has been tremendous growth in the understanding and treatment of trauma. Brain research has found neurobiological underlying layers for different trauma conditions and stress symptoms. According to the DSM-5, the trauma- and stressor-related disorders category includes disorders in which exposure to a traumatic or stressful event is listed explicitly as a diagnostic criterion. These include reactive attachment disorder, disinhibited social engagement disorder, post-traumatic stress disorder (PTSD), acute stress disorder, and adjustment disorders. The DSM-5 explains that exposure to a traumatic event can result in well-understood symptoms like anxiety and fear. However, many individuals who have been exposed to traumatic or stressful events experience other traumatic symptoms, such as an inability to experience pleasure (anhedonia), distressing feelings of unhappiness, external anger, aggression, and dissociations.[10] The DSM-5 also emphasizes that the clinical expression of these traumatic stressors frequently follows exposure to a catastrophic or aversive event.[11]

It is important to distinguish and differentiate trauma from post-traumatic stress disorder. The key is the word "post." The 2013 DSM-5 moved the diagnosis of PTSD from the anxiety disorders category to a new trauma and stress-related disorder category. Like trauma, PTSD includes exposure to actual or threatening death, serious injury, or sexual violence. But for a PTSD diagnosis, a client must manifest malfunctioning or disorder due to the presence of one or more intrusive symptoms associated with the traumatic events. Additionally, the PTSD client will experience persistent avoidance of stimuli associated with the traumatic event and will have marked alterations in arousal and reactivity associated with the traumatic event. This diagnostic also includes the negative alterations in cognitions and mood associated with the traumatic event. By contrast, a person experiencing trauma suffers an emotional response to a terrible event, but they are not "disordered" by the trauma.

This is a very important distinction. To clarify, let's discuss and compare my father's and my own stressful experiences. I suffered several traumatic life stressors around the physical absence of my father, the incarceration of my brother, and the sudden death of my sister, who died from a brain aneurism and a blood clot in September 2000. I endured these losses and eventually grew from them and learned to reconcile my emotions to these losses. My father's experiences and memories during his service to our country in the Korean War were different. His traumas persisted years after his honorable discharge. The Detroit Revolts activated an arousal and debilitating reactivity that were directly associated with the trauma he experienced in the Korean War. Both his and mine were responses to trauma, but my father experienced the revolts as a danger equal to the dangers he experienced in Korea. His response was a disorder or a post-trauma stress disorder.

Given that my father's trauma also entailed a socio-race component, I would, in addition, diagnose him with complex post-traumatic stress disorder (CPTSD). The term "complex trauma" refers to the pervasive impact of exposure to multiple or prolonged traumatic events. Complex trauma typically involves exposure to sequential or simultaneous occurrences of maltreatment. Maltreatment includes psychological injury, neglect, physical and sexual abuse, and domestic violence. Exposure to sequential stressful experiences, such as racism, casteism, sexism, and classism, can manifest in a client as complex trauma, particularly when emotional abnormality, loss of safety, direction, and/or the ability to detect or respond to danger cues are the result.

The International Classification of Diseases, 11th revision (ICD-11)[12] chose not to take a diagnostic approach, but rather chose a clinically usable approach in defining PTSD. It offered two trauma disorders: post-traumatic stress disorder and complex post-traumatic stress disorder. Both PTSD and CPTSD are stress disorders, and a client can be diagnosed with one or the other, but not both.[13] In the ICD-11, CPTSD was constructed from clinical observations of individuals with chronic, repeated, and prolonged traumas, such as sexual abuse or domestic violence. By constructing the disorder based on observed clients, the ICD-11 found that CPTSD clients displayed more complex reactions to their trauma than individuals with PTSD. Like the DSM-5, in the ICD-11, PTSD diagnosis includes reexperiencing, avoiding, and sensing current traumatic threat.

The ICD-11 CPTSD diagnosis included the three core elements of PTSD plus three pervasive additional disturbances in self-organization that occur across a variety of contexts. These self-organization disturbances are emotion regulation difficulties (problems calming down), negative self-concept (beliefs about self as worthless), and relationship difficulties (avoidance of relationships). For example, after the Detroit Revolt my father suffered from a deep sense of worthlessness and had severe challenges maintaining relationships.

Considering the advances and complexities of treating these complex and challenging stress disorders, it is prudent for mental health counselors to give their clients' trauma experiences special attention. Logic and experience suggest that counselors would do well to maximize counseling effectiveness by perfecting the four therapeutic components: therapeutic relationship and alliance; agreement on counseling task; mutual acceptance of the presenting problem; and agreement on processes and procedures. Optimizing relational techniques and evidence-based principles is critical to effective treatment of trauma and complex trauma. Trauma clients continually reexperience, avoid, and sense their trauma, and clients suffering with complex trauma also have difficulties dealing with the memories of the chronic, repeated, and prolonged emotional pain; emotional flashbacks; toxic shame; self-abandonment; social anxiety; and a harsh inner critic. It is widely accepted that complex trauma symptoms are worse in clients who experienced sexual abuse or domestic violence. Successful treatment with this population requires the therapist to be skilled in techniques that can address problems of identity, emotional self-regulation, relationships, substance abuse, dissociation, and self-injurious behaviors.[14]

Race, caste, ethnicity, skin color, gender, and poverty are life-stressors associated with trauma and complex trauma. Prolonged exposure to these stressors classifies them as immutable characteristics; they possess the potential to produce severe trauma and complex trauma disorders. Counselors treating ALANAs and clients belonging to other marginalized groups therefore must be committed to providing mental health treatment that includes complex trauma symptoms when the trauma collides with racism, casteism, sexism, and/or classism. A consideration of the intersectionality of race, caste, class, and gender must be included when analyzing the impact and experiences of racial, caste, and cultural traumas on women and ALANAs. A considerable number of ALANA clients served by mental health professionals carry scars of traumatic experiences derived from an existence of marginalization and discrimination because of race, caste, gender, and class affiliations, and these socio-cultural contexts can boost the influence of interpersonal traumatic events such as childhood abuse and domestic violence. For ALANAs, traumatic experiences shaped by oppressive social structures are everyday occurrences. These experiences must not be ignored by mental health professionals.

Histories of stress-based life events that lead to trauma exist for every trauma client. ALANAs, however, have the specific stress-based reality of living day after day in a racist, caste-based, sexist, and classist society. We find that stressors such as race and caste are known to routinely overwhelm and overburden ALANA clients. Hearing racist innuendoes, being ogled by men on the streets, being told to stay in your place, and slaving long hours for minimum wages can amount to race-based, caste-based, gender-based, and class-based stressors or traumatic events that must be addressed in counseling. The prevalence of ongoing, generational, enduring race, caste, gender, and/or class oppression are matters that often need to be addressed with ALANA clients who have experienced trauma.

Effective mental health treatment with ALANAs is hindered by a lack of complex trauma diagnoses and the acceptance of causal factors of racism, casteism, sexism, and classism because a racist, caste-based, sexist, and classist society does not want to admit that it is racist, caste-based, sexist, and classist. It is psychologically easier to dismiss the impact of race, caste, and sexism on trauma than it is to develop consensually agreed-on criteria for trauma-based counseling informed by race, caste, gender, and class. Additionally, some ALANA clients do not want to face or admit the depth of their situation; they dismiss the impact of trauma when the climate is too threatening, dangerous, or embarrassing to confront.

The determination of race-based and caste-based trauma is left to subjective interpretation rather than its objective reality.[15] However, when a counselor considers race and caste events in an ALANA client's life—events that cause traumatic reexperiencing, avoiding, sensing, arousal, and cognitive challenges—this condition must be diagnosed as trauma, if not complex trauma.

My mind still replays an episode that happened late one night when I was a graduate student at the university and my wife coached the women's volleyball team there. My wife drove the team to games in one of the university's minibuses; I would pick her up at the transportation terminal when she returned. On the night of this incident, it was raining heavily, so I went to the terminal early to be sure I would be there when she arrived to turn in the bus. As I sat in our car, in a legal parking space on the street, I noticed a university police car cruise by several times. Suddenly, there was a hard knock on the driver's window. There stood a white police officer with his gun drawn, ordering me out of the car. Having grown up Black in America, I already had my driver's license and student identification card in my hand. I placed the ID cards against the window and said I was a graduate student waiting for my wife, the volleyball coach, to return the bus to the terminal. He yelled back for me to move my car, saying I could not park there. Though the officer was clearly wrong, I moved my car.

When I mentioned this incident to my faculty and fellow students, it was minimized and ignored. Those in authority defended the actions of the police and ignored the fear and frustration that I felt. It was their opinion that I was wrong for parking and that it was the officer's duty to keep the university safe from wrongdoers. All I was asking for was empathy and understanding that my life was threatened at my school. I wanted them to ask the question, if I had been white, would the officer have pulled his weapon? Would he have even stopped and told me to move? That incident occurred in the late 1980s, and to this day I am thankful to be alive.

Typically, ALANAs are ignored, blamed, or silenced when they reveal the oppression they have experienced. Their traumas are minimized and belittled. We mental health professionals need to suppress our inclinations to shame and blame those seeking our mental health services. It is to our shame and detriment as mental health providers if we give only tacit attention to the impact of traumatic events on any vulnerable client, whatever their status in our society.

Sometimes art portrays reality better than a straight description. For example, in the movie *Snowpiercer* the Earth's remaining inhabitants are confined on a train with multiple cars. The train circles the globe as the people struggle to survive. The wealthiest passengers live in the front of the train, while the poorest live in the end car as slaves because they are stowaways. The train is a metaphor for our society: the wealthy live in luxury and the poor slave for a living. The train is owned by a billionaire, and those who paid to board the train live lavishly, having armed guards, plenty of food, and comfortable compartments in which to live and sleep. The police force on the train keeps the social order and punishes protestors. The movie does a powerful job of metaphorically reflecting our social structures and presents people who are injured because of torture, neglect, and social condition. It alludes to the impact and devastation of racism, casteism, sexism, and classism on the most vulnerable passengers on the train. *Snowpiercer* depicts the effects of abuse and neglect perpetrated by the most powerful on the least powerful. There is even a storyline of a poor child being taken to the engine car and manipulated to climb into the engine compartment to physically hold the mechanism that controls the engine in place. When the child weakens and drops the mechanism, they are crushed by the engine and they die.

I have found that using a movie like *Snowpiercer* in my supervision and training of mental health professionals helps them to see their clients, specifically ALANA clients, in the light of their traumas. It gives them a space in which to acknowledge the victimization and injustice their clients are reporting. Movies such as *Snowpiercer* give the counselor the emotional space to visualize their ALANA clients on that train, destined to crash or run out of fuel. Awareness activities such as watching relevant media presentations can not only enhance sensitivity but can prevent a counselor minimizing the risk and harm of inadequately treating trauma sufferers, particularly if the trauma is complicated by abuse, neglect, racism, sexism, or classism. It is too costly for the therapist to turn a blind eye to human suffering. People can literally and metaphorically die from trauma, complex trauma, or benign neglect. Let me say more about this last condition.

A major hinderance to effective treatment of ALANAs suffering from trauma and complex trauma is benign neglect. That is, ALANA trauma and complex trauma experiences are often conceptualized as mild and unthreatening. Mental health professionals often expect ALANAs to be accustomed to suffering and thereby ignore the severity of their distress. Americans who downplay racial-caste trauma are not intentionally minimizing the suffering of ALANAs with race-caste trauma. Rather, they are responding out of a worldview that has minimized and marginalized ALANAs for generations. Americans from the dominant caste do not have a stellar history and legacy of valuing ALANAs. History has also revealed that dominant-caste Americans often remain silent and complicit to the trauma and complex trauma that race-caste existence perpetrates on ALANAs. Dominant-caste Americans do not want to admit that there is systemic racism, casteism, sexism, and classism. They often express that America does not suffer from these problems—that they are issues from the past. It seems that dominant-caste Americans are suffering from cognitive dissonance where race is concerned. They want to believe that America is fair to all citizens, but they know this supposition is not true. Even when recognizing disparities, those in the dominant caste do not want to give up their privileges to enable a just and equitable society for all persons. The ongoing disparity creates an unhealthy society for everyone.

Dominant-caste Americans are taught that life is equal, fair, and autocratic, so they should not have to give up their "hard-earned" advantages. They do not want to accept that, as great and wonderful as America is, there exists in the fabric of America a shapeshifting, unspoken, race-based caste pyramid.[16] Most Americans would agree that white America has for centuries used and abused ALANAs, women, and the poor. But it is difficult to accept that our country is racist and caste conscious at its core. Dominant-caste Americans can admit that racism and casteism exist, but they prefer to focus on how their ancestors arrived on this continent with little to nothing and transformed the United States into a world-class economy based purely on grit and rugged individualism.

As mental health professionals, we cannot treat people based on what we have been taught, believe, or think should be their plight. Instead, we must move past our cognitive biases and treat people based on their treatment needs. Trauma and complex trauma have their own inner logic that is self-maintaining, self-perpetuating, and self-condemning. We must practice a more just and equitable way of healing. While treating clients with trauma and complex trauma, we must wonder about and explore why our clients do not give up and do not commit suicide. Understanding what makes them resilient is key. To deepen my understanding of resilience, I have developed the habit of an annual summer ritual of reading Viktor E. Frankl's *Man's Search for Meaning* as a refresher on how to care, love, and survive suffering. Frankl's book helps me explore this issue and reinforces ways to care for trauma and complex trauma clients. We must discover and rediscover how our mental health clients are resilient and retain a deep commitment to life. We must understand that honest and succinct conversations and treatment addressing the underlying issues of trauma and complex trauma will lead to life, not death. It is the denial of and resistance to the severity of the disorder that leads to dysfunction and death.

Frankl, who suffered during the Holocaust, called us to adjust our understanding of trauma and complex trauma. He instructed us to focus on the frustration of the will and the quest for meaning. He suggested that we focus on the force beyond our control and allow this judicious choosing to empower our responses to traumatic situations. Those of us in the helping profession must continually remember that we cannot control what happens to us or our clients (stimulus), but we can seek to help clients control what we/they feel about the stimulus and thus more consciously and efficaciously influence our/their responses to the stimulus and situation. When something tragic happens, perhaps what's most important is how we respond. We can turn inward and retreat from this world, or we can try to do what we can to make it a better place. When trauma, such as death, abuse, racism, or sexism, visits our world, we can retreat or do what Frankl did: find hope and meaning in the trauma.

Again, I am not suggesting that people pull themselves up by their bootstraps. A common saying is, "God helps those who help themselves." In a worldly sort of way, this phase may be considered wise, but in most spiritual situations it is not completely true. Scripture clearly says, in many ways, that God helps those who trust in God, not those who help themselves (Proverbs 3:5–6). And our experience with God often comes through humans.

What we need are more humans who understand the relationship between race and trauma. The experiences of racism (as well as sexism and classism) have negatively impacted women and men of color in traumatic ways that have resulted in depression, anxiety, and other mental health problems. As a therapist, I have frequently confronted powerlessness, entrapment, pain, confusion, and loss among my clients. This trauma was exacerbated when interacting with racism, rape, physical and psychological assaults, and domestic violence. The interaction resulted in an increase in physical and emotional distress and disruptions.[17]

As I am sure is true for many others, I have come to terms with the inevitability of suffering and of the trauma that may result. Thus, it is critical to help clients of mental health services realize that they must possess a drive to survive and persist despite the traumas in their lives. Our wounds show themselves in many ways, but holding on to these wounds and celebrating their victories over us—by continuing to suffer—is an unnecessary tragedy. Clients must be helped to persist through their traumatic state even when they fail in their attempts to heal. If we surrender to our traumas, we make them captains over our souls. A healthier goal is to become more patient, loving, hopeful, faithful, and compassionate with our whole life experience.

As a therapist, I had treated trauma victims, but I was confronted with enormous amounts of trauma in my roles as a supervisor and psychologist with a local community mental health agency, as clinical supervisor for a methadone clinic, and as a pastoral psychotherapist missionary to a Haitian community. In these settings, I found myself immersed with clients and communities who were dealing with trauma and complex trauma more deeply and intensely than I had witnessed before. I remember confronting this level of trauma early in my counseling career when I worked with a severely suicidal client. On a gut level, I felt that her depression had a deep underlying root. As we discussed her childhood and adolescence, her abuse and trauma experiences were exposed.

I clearly recall the shift in my thinking and practice that was critical to treating patients. This shift was to a trauma-informed service system that included two major components: creating an environment that is emotionally and physically safe for therapeutic work and incorporating evidence-based, trauma-specific knowledge, skills, and strategies in all aspects of service delivery and practice.[18] Without this type of approach, the client will often be unable to persist in treatment and will be inclined to run head-long into another traumatic experience or another oppressive system. To restate the obvious, truly competent trauma-informed services must adopt an overarching comprehensive approach that takes into consideration trauma-related issues in all aspects of clinical care.[19]

Serving in the trenches with ALANAs has enabled me to see the effects of complex trauma in a truly clinical manner. ALANA clients often develop ideas, beliefs, actions, and behaviors that collude with racism. This collusion with racism is termed "internalized oppression" or "internalized racism."

Internalized Oppression and Attachment Theory

Internalized racism occurs when ALANAs overlook their socio-racial victimization experiences and behave in a manner that colludes with the oppressive victimization. To defend against these internalized feelings, emotions, memories, and so forth, the ALANA uses psychological defenses to place the painful experience into the unconscious system. The ALANA who experienced the oppression, personally and/ or communally, works against their own interest by defending and colluding with the oppressor and victimizer to the detriment of the wellbeing of their own people. This colluding behavior feeds intracultural and multicultural conflicts and maintains unhealthy hierarchies.[20]

When racism is internalized a racial group oppressed by racism supports the supremacy and dominance of the dominant group. This support is welcomed and rewarded by the oppressor who maintains the set of attitudes, behaviors, social structures, and ideologies that undergird the dominating group's power and privilege, limiting the oppressed group's own advantages. Internalized racism is an internal assault on the persons of ALANAs. More than just a consequence of racism, internalized racism is a systemic reaction to racism that has a life of its own. It is a manifestation of the relationship among racism, white privilege, Black inferiority, and white supremacy, and it prevents

ALANAs from experiencing their full humanity, power, and abilities to participate as co-creators of a free and equitable society.

History is replete with examples of internalized racism and its effects and consequences on ALANAs. One prominent and well-known example of internalized racism would be the slave who betrayed Denmark Vesey, a Black American carpenter in Charleston, South Carolina and founding member of the African Methodist Episcopal church in that city. In 1822, Vesey was identified by a slave as the leader of a planned slave revolt. Some readers may agree with the slave snitching and informing officials of Vesey's plans. Others may feel that the slave acted in his own interest and received a reward for his betrayal, thus seeing his actions as reasonable and not internalized oppression. However, it is difficult to argue that it was to the benefit of Black Americans in 1822 for thirty-six slaves to be executed and thousands of other slaves to continue in slavery because of perks to one slave informant.

This type of betrayal resulting from internalized oppression is another important concept and phenomenon for the clinician to consider in treating trauma and complex trauma. I will never forget the supervision work I did with a young African American male counselor who could not work effectively with young African American men. He could not trust them: he felt they were malingering and acting out against the system no matter how much contradictory data the family presented. He always believed the negative reports from the courts and schools. But because something deep within him cared for the young men he treated, he sought out supervision to help him resolve the internal conflict.

He and I began to explore times that he felt betrayed by the system and times he felt betrayed by his people. His anger toward both Black and white culture became a focus of supervision. We focused on the posing and posturing that he did to distinguish himself from the African American clients he treated. It became clear that he had a deep resentment for his African American self and was embarrassed by it and wanted to justify his position as a middle-class mental health professional. When he finally confessed in supervision that he was embarrassed to be Black and identified where these feelings originated, he was able to eventually overcome this internalized oppression and effectively treat young male African American clients.

Internalized oppression is very closely connected to relationship complication due to attachment difficulties. The issue of attachment is another critical lesson learned from the trenches of complex trauma work with ALANAs. Because of the interpersonal and intrapersonal aspects of the complex trauma experience, attachment bonds and abilities to establish effective trusting relationships are impacted. Attachment theory indicates that it is critical for individuals to develop and seek closeness from family members, find a haven among caregivers, a secure attachment bond with guardians, a non-fear and non-anxiety-based separation from family, and a healthy range of grief and sorrow upon the absence of a caregiver.

Attachment theory is best defined by investigating the Secure, Avoidant, Ambivalent, and Disorganized (SAAD) attachment paradigm (see Figure 2.1).[21] According to attachment theory, one develops a secure, avoidant, ambivalent, or disorganized attachment based on the interactions between caregivers and the self. Based on a person's interactions with their early caregivers, they will develop a positive or negative sense of self and of others. By combining the four possible interactions of the self and others, a four-category table emerges (Figure 2.1). According to this theory, the combined beliefs about the self and the other shape our expectations about future relationships. Our early attachment serves as a lens through which we see relationships and people. This lens informs us about how to function in intimate relationships, and it informs our attachment style.

A healthy attachment promotes feelings of safety, trust, comfort, and assurance in human beings, and it exhibits warmth when a loved one returns. A healthy attachment allows people to delay gratification and respond to direction and wise counsel. Conversely, an unhealthy attachment, which typically results from an attachment injury, is seen in an insecure attachment bond. As stated previously, emotional problems such as identity, emotional self-regulation, relationships, substance abuse, dissociation, and self-injurious behaviors can be the consequence of attachment and trauma interactions. Adding the additional stressors of attachment difficulties (such as identity disorganization, identification with aggressors, faulty assumptions, distressed relationships, and reality distortions) to trauma and complex trauma compounds the stressful situation.

As a therapist, I find that trauma victims with attachment injuries are more likely to present with soul wounds. Soul wounds are injuries to persons that hinder them from connecting interpersonally. Clients with soul wounds reject attempts by others to repair relationships; they cycle through pushes and pulls, moving close and then rejecting loved ones. Soul-wounded clients also tend to have fragmented relationships that are weakened by their attachment injury.

In addition to attachment injuries, the therapist must also attend to heart injuries. Heart injuries, soul wounds, and attachment problems in complex trauma clients often reveal themselves as bruised hearts, performance-based hearts, hardened hearts, or addicted hearts. A bruised heart or shattered heart is a client who is unable to contain the love others give. The love of others appears to flow right through the injured patient. The heart is so injured and bruised that the patient avoids the sensation of real feelings. Performance-based hearts exist in individuals who feel they must be good behaviorally and meet certain performance standards to be loved. These patients believe that if they do not live up to certain standards and rules to earn the love of others, they will be found unworthy and discarded. People with hardened hearts operate as if they are not worthy of love, and the fear of abandonment causes the person to close their heart to love and affection. They do not accept love, and they do not believe that others will truly love them without ulterior motives. Addicted hearts lead to love addiction, codependency, and emotionally neglectful behaviors. Individuals with addicted hearts are frequently manipulative, unfaithful in relationships, and prone to dependence of one kind or another. Because of my father-absence, I developed a performance-based heart. I have thus spent years performing to get affection and attention, caught in a perpetual pattern of doing good and being good in the search for acceptance.

My father was physically absent but psychologically present. As a Black man on a white university campus, I was embarrassed to not have been raised by my father; to not know where my father was or how he was doing was even more painful. It was not until we reconciled during my final year in seminary that my father/soul wound began to heal. From our brief conversations together, I stopped experiencing him as good or bad and began to love him as the man that he was. In this process, I gained a deep appreciation of his struggles and his victories. My father died shortly after our reconciliation, and even though he was permanently physically absent, the psychological health we established allowed me to accept his humanity and the realities of his strengths and weaknesses.

My healing from my father wound was aided by my relationship with my life partner. My wife would hold my face, kiss my nose, and tell me how much she loved my father's nose. Her love and my new perspective and insight into my father's pain allowed me to accept the blessing that I am very much like my father and have accomplished the dreams he had for himself. I have found peace and a rich inner life from my journey to wholeness around the complicated trauma of my father and my father wound.

This racial trauma experience of being abandoned by my African American father became very real for me after my clinical internship, when my family was packing to move from Philadelphia, Pennsylvania to Richmond, Virginia. I discovered and read for the first time a letter my father had written me seven years prior to this move. In the letter my father explained the racial trauma he had experienced in the Korean War and the years of struggle after the Detroit

Revolt. He explained that he was undergoing bio-feedback treatment from a psychologist and realized that he now knew his true calling—to become a clinical psychologist. At the time he wrote the letter, I was a youth pastor. When I read the letter seven years later, I was completing the last requirement on the road to earning my degree in counseling psychology. Three years later I was licensed by the Commonwealth of Virginia as a clinical psychologist.

I have come a long way from my trauma experiences in Detroit, Michigan. Through counseling I have processed my own demons, and through formal training I have learned to "do" psychology and to effectively treat trauma clients. As do other therapists, I seek to differentiate trauma experiences conceptually and programmatically, distinguishing diagnoses such as PTSD and complex trauma. Recognizing what was previously broken in the treatment of trauma and race, we trauma-informed therapists apply our skills and knowledge to treating trauma among ALANAs, factoring in the complications of socio-race, gender, sexism, classism, and racism.

Part II

HEALING AND PRACTICE

4

CHALLENGING BARRIERS

INTERSECTIONALITY IS JUST one conceptual frame to use in the effective treatment of racial trauma. Many mental health professionals spend their careers testing existing norms and procedures of healing. Practitioners entering this helping field bring with them new approaches to healing, built on the perspectives of those who taught and mentored them. The proverb, "Standing up on your shoulders I can see twice as far as you saw" expresses this.

With this enhanced line of sight, counseling interventions are improved as they incorporate "true" history around race, eradicate inequities, and utilize previously successful strategies to obtain restoration and reparation.[1] While these issues are important to some, others view them as unnecessary and irrelevant.[2] In the end, healing practices that do not consider the role of racial trauma must be judged inadequate. Racial trauma is implicit in the experiences of many ALANAs.

The Missed Opportunity

Some years ago, at a mid-Atlantic urban university, a white psychologist sought consultation from a Black colleague after a counseling session with an African American cis-gendered married couple. The couple had been married for ten years. They were college educated and both working on master's degrees. The counselor reported that he asked the couple to share their most complicated life struggle with him. They presented their joint unhappiness around their financial situation, explaining that they had no savings and were expecting no inheritance because of generational poverty caused by racism, redlining, and other race-based economic barriers. This counselor was surprised by the couples' pain, anger, and disenfranchisement. He assumed that the couple would present like most white couples he had counseled. Instead of anchoring his intervention around their presented problem, the counselor focused on their communication difficulties (e.g., unmet needs, unfulfilled wants, and communication exercises).

The couple continued to communicate that their problems were a result of racist government policies and racial oppression. They discussed how affirmative action policies left them feeling blamed and vulnerable when they returned home to family and friends who had fewer opportunities than they did and suffered more financially. As the couple continued to redirect the counselor toward their real concerns, the counselor described them as being overwhelmed by projections and preoccupied by cultural mistrust. Further, the psychologist began to perceive the couple as unauthentic and antagonistic. He felt that they were acting in a dysfunctional and inappropriate learned helpless manner. If not for the fact that he felt the suggestion would have been insulting, the psychologist would have recommended biweekly intensive psychotherapy. The counselor at last confessed that he was unable to shift his orientation and methodology toward a "more" helpful counseling approach and thus desired to refer the couple for therapy to a counselor skilled in addressing racial trauma.

During consultation, this counselor and his colleague consultant explored the norms and procedures for success during his sessions with the couple. They examined the potential meanings underlying the counselor's inability to connect and develop an alliance with the couple. They investigated the reasons that the counselor felt so trapped and ill-prepared to treat the couple and discussed what hindered him from entering their world. The counselor disclosed that he struggled with the challenge of entering the "Black experience." He was not comfortable nuancing the subtleties, survival experiences, and coping strategies of being Black. He felt neither qualified nor invited to help this couple process their racial experiences.

Any counselor must reconcile incongruences between their conscious and unconscious thinking and intuition. Philosophically, a counselor's presuppositions, biases, and theoretical and political orientation affect counselor impact. Multicultural knowledge, awareness, skills, and experiences are also critical to counseling clients who have experienced or are experiencing socio-racial trauma. In the case above, the counselor and the consultant wrestled with the complexities of his unconscious mind and how it interacted with his conscious mind and behaviors. Consciously, he knew that the couple was highly intelligent and middle class. But their counseling sessions presented the race-based traumatic experiences of two Black people. This incongruence evoked in the counselor a negative unconscious response of which he was not proud.

Through his consultation, the counselor realized that his presuppositions about human nature were highjacked by the disenfranchisement seated before him. He realized that there was something deeper and very important to which he was not attending. He was not referring to the supernatural unconscious referenced by Sigmund Freud. Rather, his understanding reflects the work of Wilhelm Wundt and William James, who conceptualized the mind as an instrument that creates models of our world and the brain, through our detecting senses.

The mind-brain concept is critical to effective counseling around race and trauma. Our mind-brain is a two-tier processing system. Our conscious brain senses and receives, and our unconscious mind fills in the blanks when information is incomplete. The counselor had a conscious processing of the couple "on paper" and an unconscious internal processing of the Black couple in the counseling room. The couple presented in counseling differently from what the counselor read of their biography. In the room they shared hurt experienced over generations. They discussed familial financial history that included parents being shipped to family members in the North to gain better opportunities. They processed issues grounded in the traumas of a mother-in-law who, because of her race and impoverished upbringing, told the wife to never "trust any man with your money." This couple discussed generational racial trauma tracing back to the husband's grandfather, who was destroyed by urban renewal and redlining. The couple in the room had experienced a great deal of personal and communal racial trauma around finances, information not included in their biographical summary. Their generational racial trauma was triggered in the counseling but left unprocessed, producing internal conflict in both the couple and the counselor. The couple found a trusting and supportive counselor who, unfortunately, was ill-prepared (although experientially equipped) to handle their pain and story. The counselor was not an overt racist or a classist; however, the unexpected and undiagnosed intersectionality of race and trauma in the couple triggered an unconscious race-based conclusion in the counselor. He concluded, rightly or wrongly, that his unconscious mind was not prepared for the energy and vulnerability he would need to effectively counsel this Black couple on their Black trauma issues. The counselor was afraid that if he had focused on the couple's underlying racial trauma, it might have triggered a fight, flight, or freeze reaction.[3] During consultation, however, the consultant pushed the counselor to consider his own upbringing as a poor, white, rural man. That experience came with its own trauma. From this vantage point, the consultant argued, the counselor was able to enter a healing cross-cultural trauma conversation with the couple. Even if the couple was triggered by entering a conversation around racial trauma, the counselor's consultant assured him he was equipped to help them process that pain.

After several consultations developing the strategy of directly assessing the couple's racial trauma experiences, the counselor returned to his work with the couple. When the wife disclosed that she was deeply wounded by the traumas of her mother as her mother was never welcomed or loved by her family and hated her own father, the counselor affirmed and listened. As the counselor probed these experiences, the wife shared how her mother's trauma was connected to her grand-mother and the pains they both experienced raising thirteen and eight children respectively in a racially oppressive Southern community. The wife realized she carried this generational trauma into her marriage. She further connected it to her trauma around being teased for her dark complexion and full-body shape. For the first time, she revealed to her husband that she was gang-raped as a young woman.

The husband knew some of his wife's racial trauma history and carried it alongside his own. He felt guilty for not being able to help his wife reconcile her distrust of men, particularly him. But, as his wife expressed the reasons for her discomfort around men, he realized her discomfort was not about him. He was then able to share with his wife that he was also teased for his African features and ostracized for his academic exceptionalism. He also mourned the unresolved death of his father and the difficult relationship he had with his stepfather.

Treating clients with racial trauma is especially challenging for counselors not trained in this area. The counselor treating the Black couple struggled to address their racial trauma because he was discon-nected from his own trauma. As counselors who accompany ALANAs through despair, we must master the art of helping them remain hopeful.[4] This difficult work is that of a wounded healer,[5] a counselor aware of their injuries and equipped to walk through the shadows of another. Wounded healing embraces one's brokenness as a threshold to entering the counseling relationship, particularly around racial trauma. Counseling racially traumatized clients is not a supernatural under-taking, but it does require training the unconscious mind to experience and automatically respond to unknown human conditions.[6]

By its nature, counseling is a profession that requires working with clients in crisis. Unfortunately, psychotherapy originated in an era of interpersonal aloofness and taught counselors to remain impar-tial and distant. This forced neutrality does not promote a counselor using their personal experiences as a counseling instrument. Here is where counselors need to draw on their unconscious capacities. The conscious thoughts of a counselor are helpful with structured didactic tasks,[7] but because of the massive amounts of information we process as humans, our unconscious mind automatically intakes and processes data without bringing it all to conscious awareness. Thus, when counseling deeply wounded people (such as racially traumatized people), counselors need strategies that allow them to respond to information not shared.

Years ago, my counseling supervisor, Dr. Carl Whitaker,[8] forced me to use and respect my unconscious. While I was counseling a family of four, Whitaker was observing my session through a one-way mirror. He called me out of the session and said, "Young man, I don't know who that counselor is in the room with that family. Trust your gut, man. Have that family appreciate and experience who they are by connecting with them and drawing them in." Returning to the session, I shifted our focus to the dynamics of relationships. Encouraged by my conversation with my supervisor, I shared that I was a trauma survivor and the effect that trauma had on my life. Based on their knowing responses, I sensed that the family was "stuck" in dysfunction because they were deeply wounded. I began inquiring and holding conversations with the family around their prior relationships, with an openness to trauma and racially traumatic experiences. The very vocal and powerful mother mentioned that, as a child and a young woman, she was teased about her size and her dark complexion. She mentioned the abuse from her previous husband and the pain around her not being able to conceive a child with him. This mother informed her family that her first husband had blamed her for their marital problems and belittled her as a woman. Her daughter, who was adopted, shared that she understood because she had been abused while with a foster family. Her son got up from his seat and hugged his mother.

The father sat emotionally paralyzed during his wife's and daughter's tearful disclosures. Noticing his discomfort, I asked him to share with his family what he was experiencing. He then began to share the story of his first marriage. This father disclosed that previously he was married to a white woman he had met in the military. He stated that, at first, she loved him and they were very happy, but after the birth of their son, their relationship changed. His first wife became rageful and abusive to him and their son. Initially, she would just yell and shout, but gradually she began to slap and hit. He explained that her anger was connected to the African American features of his son and the rejection of their family by the wife's family. The father further stated that he took the abuse until she hurt their son, which is when he and his son moved out. During this conversation the son just sat in the room with his chin in his hands and looked at his father. It was the first time he had heard the details of his and his father's abuse. When his father began to cry, the son cautiously put his hand on his father's knee.

As a result of our conversations, we named our counseling space as a healing space. We uncovered that the parents were struggling with feelings of inadequacy and vulnerability that were being manifested in the behavior of their children. The counseling focus switched from the scapegoated child to the dynamic dysfunction within the executive system—to the impact of racial trauma on the executive system and the sibling system. Our work together became a growing space around our traumas. I did not speak in depth about my traumas but used metaphors and spiritual analogies to ground their stories in hope, reconciliation, and healing. As I have revisited my time with this family over the years, I believe that I owe them tremendous gratitude for allowing me to walk with them into, through, and out of their racial trauma experiences.

Dr. Whitaker's advice on being human and connecting with the family around their problem freed me to let my true self occupy the necessary healing place in a family system. My supervisor was instructing me to be a healing presence. Years of reflecting on his teaching and integrating his theories has equipped me to work with honesty and integrity when addressing issues of trauma and particularly racial trauma in my preaching, teaching, and clinical practice. When counseling racially traumatized clients, it is often helpful to combine psychological knowledge with one's spiritual-cultural-experiential core beliefs. This stance encourages counselors to integrate into their therapy who they were, who they are, and who they are becoming.

Treating racially traumatized families requires an integrative counseling approach. The counselor must develop a comfort in the uncertainties and contradictions of clients' lived experiences. What's needed is a sensitivity and openness to all experiences of families and individuals brave enough to seek counseling.

Understanding Deep Time

Using the knowledge of history as a teacher ("who they were") is central to the concept of *sankofa*. *Sankofa* is an African word from the Akan tribe in Ghana. It is derived from the words *san* (return), *ko* (go), and *fa* (look, seek, and take). Together it is translated as "return to fetch what is at risk of being left behind."[9]

Sankofa-infused counseling involves a focus on "deep time," an approach that helps counselees examine the impact of their past, present, and future. Viewing a situation or choices from these angles will help the client or family be more generative and focused on the work of healing. *Sankofa*-infused counseling helps counselors listen to the client's trauma narratives and build therapeutic trust.

This is a deeper introspection approach to counseling and entails shifting the focus from solely on the client to a focus on the client, the content, the context, and story.[10] The approach entails obtaining a broad perspective of the client's entire being of mind, body, and soul. Counselors understand this all-inclusive perspective as metacognition—the simultaneous awareness of thought and process—and the perspective positions counselors to change traumatic narratives into liminal thresholds that allow counselees to envision themselves differently and overcome their blind spots.[11] Cognitive therapy is very effective in helping people understand better what they're experiencing, but understanding alone does not transform people on a deeper level; we must connect knowing with being. When you connect knowing with being, you enable experiential learning. Counseling must be more than a lecture.

Lectures of this type are described as a banking system approach to education.[12] In this type of educational system, the educator assumes that the learner is an empty cup to be filled by the educator's full pitcher. More recently, educators have called for a problem-solving approach to education, where the educator becomes a practitioner of healing and liberation by developing community through narrative and engagement.[13] In this learning orientation the educator approaches teaching from a standpoint of an awareness of race, gender, ethnicity, and class—without fearing an uncontrollable, emotional, and passion-filled classroom experience. This problem-posing approach can be effective in counseling race and trauma clients. To have lasting impact, counseling, particularly around trauma issues, must be collaborative. As educators and therapists, we must recognize that a more engaging interpersonal experience with students and clients will create classrooms and counseling office spaces that respect pain and practice liberation. A problem-solving approach will empower students and clients to arrive at an internal place where they can speak freely and openly about any subject, including abuse, trauma, manipulation, racism, sexism, and all forms of oppression.

When everyone takes seriously the experiences of others, counseling and education spaces can be ones of safety and healing. Creating this climate requires a fierce commitment to authenticity and growth to understand each other's reality and transform pain into progress. To paraphrase Freire, it is only through this type of praxis, where those who help are being helped and those being helped are helping, that we can free ourselves from oppression.

The colleague mentioned previously allowed his unconscious mind to hinder him from responding to the couple with awareness and without bias. He was a man of sorrow, one acquainted with trauma and loss. His pain was not related to his race, but his pain did position him to "join" in the racial trauma of the couple and offer a more fruitful counseling experience. This counselor genuinely valued the couple and possessed the competence to develop a strategy to deal with their pain and history in a nonantagonistic manner. But this cognitive and affective shift required him to give up his agenda and orientation. He was being challenged to operate in a flexible, uncharted, therapeutic manner. In other words, he was being internally directed to counsel the couple without knowing the outcome and explicit reason for his behaviors. The counselor needed to trust his gut over his conscious mind, a vulnerability that he saw as unacceptable because he had never tried it before. He would have benefitted from a co-therapist who could have intervened during his moments of deep doubt. The co-therapist could have outwardly processed both his and the couple's thoughts and feelings in the moment—a metacognitive activity.

Metacognitions and deep-time thinking are critical in treating issues of socio-race and trauma because our conscious and unconscious awareness affects many aspects of our lives. For instance, an individual recruited to a new employment opportunity will have both conscious and unconscious thoughts and feelings about taking a new position. Consciously, the employee may consider factors such as salary and resources. But unconsciously, they might be influenced by relationships and environmental pressures. The employee may consider the impact of the move on family. Thus, counselors working with ALANAs must consider issues of immigration, gender roles, spirituality, and childrearing practices in counseling.[14] These issues require conscious and unconscious attention, particularly if they are complicated by individual, family, or community traumatic experiences.

It is virtually impossible to effectively counsel an ALANA client, even in a vocational matter, if the client and/or the counselor are unaware of their unconscious biases around racial conflicts and racial trauma. Our unconscious awareness of the influences of our presuppositions and biases on our functioning must be addressed, particularly when it comes to addressing socio-racial trauma.

Trauma, 12-Step, and Non-12-Step Interventions

Awareness of a counselor's conscious and unconscious biases and presuppositions is extremely important when working with the mental health issue of addiction. Trauma and addiction are frequently co-occurring clinical issues for ALANA populations.[15] A familiarity with addiction counseling is a powerful primer for all healers. Counselors acquainted with Alcoholics Anonymous, Narcotics Anonymous, Adult Children of Alcoholics, or any of the addiction healing communities have seen the healing power of these organizations and are convinced of the healing power surrounding a belief in and acceptance of a Higher Power. In the language of the Church, they are using confession to assist their clients to gain serenity to accept what they cannot change, courage to change what they can, and the wisdom to know the difference.[16]

Addiction counselors are called to be full members of the communities they serve. These counselors are accountable to their addiction communities and need the community's commitment and support. Accepting the confessional truths of the Serenity Prayer[17] and 12-step program[18] positions addiction counselors to serve with their whole being, including their wounded selves,[19] and resist becoming an interrogating other.[20]

When counselors expand their practices to include addiction, the presenting issues often intersect with issues of race and trauma. The counselor must enter a community expecting confession and a "lived" addiction, trauma, and race experience. If the counselor is uncomfortable or unable to share experiences of addiction, race, and/ or trauma, they are perceived as unqualified. Counselors struggling with this phenomenon search for ways to answer these questions about their own experiences with integrity. I encountered this reality when I served as a mental health supervisor for community mental health clinics that treated patients with addiction, socio-race, trauma, and other mental health conditions. During supervision and training, I sought to help counselors develop therapeutic responses to client questions around these issues. With the goal of empowerment and providing excellent mental health treatment, we commenced supervision and training on the premise that 12-step addiction programs worked. Counselors would focus on the programs' abilities to direct the client toward truth, sobriety, power over substances, and recognition of an inner "Higher Power." Counselors without a personal history of addiction, racism, and trauma were trained in non-12-step psychotherapeutic programs. These cognitive-behavioral group therapy and social learning theory programs effectively modified drug-taking and drug-related behaviors.[21] Moreover, these non-12-step mental health addiction programs have proven very effective for over eighty years.[22] My job was to help counselors reframe the perceived inadequacy as an inherent competency.

Of course, the most effective forms of treatment for alcohol and drug use involve a combination of elements and techniques from both 12-step programs and non-12-step psychotherapeutic programs. But the most effective program at our community clinics added an additional layer when treating underlying race and trauma issues—developing coping strategies and soliciting racial traumatic stories.

I fondly recall my time leading a men's group of dual-diagnosed substance abusers (substance abuse and mental health diagnosed). Members of the groups were chronic drug users with long histories of domestic abuse, trauma from gun injuries, and/or chronic poverty. As a result of their lived experiences, racial trauma was also a constant in their lives. We used 12-step principles, motivational interviewing, and DBT in the group. From the 12-step programs we focused on the goals of abstinence, sobriety, and accountability through peer and counselor support. From motivational interviewing we used the stages of change conceptualization to encourage participants to commit to action.[23] We used DBT to address issues of race and trauma. Specifically, we taught both groups mindfulness exercises, emotional self-regulation and distress tolerance techniques, and interpersonal effectiveness as problem-solving strategies.[24]

By the indicators of reduced relapse, active attendance, and increased interpersonal effectiveness, our eclectic approach was very effective with our racially traumatized clients. Specifically, when we compared the performance and conversations of clients in the group to clients in individual counseling sessions and other counseling groups, these patients improved the most on the outcome measures. Moreover, the clients in the group reported that they felt heard and respected in ways that made them want to be better people. The norms and practices of counseling were changed by combining 12-step principles, motivational interviewing, and DBT. The group members expressed that they were comfortable with the counselor's approach and avail-ability. They felt that when they had a crisis, unlike other counseling situations, they could contact their counselor for support and stabi-lization. The group members shared that the change in format, from a tell-them-what-to-do approach to a talk-them-off-the-ledge (crisis intervention) approach, allowed them to be transparent during the counseling sessions. Although they did not like the ambiguity of the new approach, they trusted the counselor and allowed the counselor access to their real world. This type of emotional availability on the part of the counselor and the client is critical in multicultural trauma work. The vulnerability of the group members and the counselor established a trust that moved beyond substance abuse, race, class, and trauma experiences. Individual conversations with members of the men's group revealed that several men realized they were allowing the coun-selor to shepherd them much like they would a pastor. These conver-sations revealed that the men were not worried about their image or how they were perceived by other men in the group. Rather, they were concerned about using the opportunity to move beyond shame and worry to resilience. I remember a conversation with a man in the group after we watched a video of Travis Greene titled *Intentional.* The group member, who suffered from PTSD following a gunshot wound, stated that he was intentional when he was a drug dealer, and he was intentionally shot by a rival dealer. He promised that he was now going to be intentional about overcoming his physical pain and emotional problems and would intentionally move on with his life.

At an unconscious level, the group members realized that their trauma experiences were not badges of honor, but badges of shame that continued to haunt and cripple them. Unconsciously or consciously, they experienced counseling as an opportunity to act outside of their public personas and personal conditions. The group members practiced mindfulness and interpersonal effectiveness as they journeyed to their true selves. They moved a step away from their identities as drug users and moved a step closer to their identities as healthy human beings. Without conscious planning, the group members confronted their internalized racism and generational race trauma. That is, the men didn't have to define themselves as what some called "an inevitable statistic"—a Black male on the road to incarceration. For a season, they stopped living risky and dangerous lives because they perceived the group space as safe space. They removed their mask of oppression and for an hour a week interacted with the counselor at the intersection of their pain and peace.

The group members did not need to be vulnerable to experience joy; they needed to be vulnerable to experience their pain. These men faced their adversities and failures together with the group and counselor. They found the courage to confront their fears of addiction, poverty, abuse, and violence. Many were transformed into new selves that no longer needed approval or feared reprisal.

Over my years as a psychologist, pastor, and professor, I have learned that many ALANAs would benefit from counseling and mentoring with counselors who support their brave examinations of pain and trauma around matters of race and racism. It is critical to create healing spaces that engender vulnerability and allow the injured to be their true selves and to triumph over their pain. Unfortunately, these healing spaces are rare. However, when traumatized clients encounter this type of rare space, they are enabled to emotionally visit generational trauma and confront grief, anger, and sadness.

As a therapist who often worked with African American adolescent young men, I was deeply moved by Kalen Davis's portrayal of Shawn Campbell in the TV series *Shots Fired*, directed by Gina Prince-Bythewood. The issues of race and trauma are at the center of this show, and Prince-Bythewood skillfully presents the complexities surrounding them. In the show Shawn's older brother Cory is killed by a white police officer and framed as a drug dealer. Shawn and his mother (Shameeka Campbell) are presented along with a white mother (Alicia Carr), whose son, a white college student, is killed by Deputy Joshua Beck, a Black police officer. Prince-Bythewood holds up a mirror to the race and trauma experiences of the characters in her show. Throughout the season, Shawn's grief over the murder of and the injustice done to his brother is complicated by his desire to lessen his mother's pain, remain a model student, and develop his own identity as a young Black man. But it is not easy to move past the trauma their family experienced.

Young ALANAs are looking for identity, belonging, and purpose. Many of them continue to be confused about who they are, who they belong to, and what is their purpose. Early in my career I was engaged in this work to compensate for the imprisonment of my biological brother. Now I realize that I was created and nurtured for this calling.

While serving as an associate professor of psychology, I received funding to pilot a program titled, "The BEST (Brothers, Energized, Spirited, Talented) Program." This program became a component of my Helping Relations service-learning course. The course was intended for university students strongly considering a career in a human services field, such as psychology, social work, nursing, medicine, or teaching, and involved the students learning about counseling while participating in activities designed to meet the mental health needs of African American and Latino American male elementary school students in an after-school program. The course was designed to offer a situated learning experience to students through cultural emersion, multicultural helping,[25] and coaching with elementary school students. Students applied what they were learning in the classroom to the after-school program. The university students were required to read Janice E. Hale's *Learning While Black: Creating Educational Excellence for African American Children*, Dan Millman's *Way of the Peaceful Warrior*, Don Miguel Ruiz's *The Four Agreements*, and Malcolm Gladwell's *Blink: The Power of Thinking without Thinking*. Twice a week the child participants were bussed from their school to a church campus. Our community partners were a public county elementary school and a suburban African American Baptist church. The elementary students in the program were all classified as at-risk. They were academically behind in school, and their trajectories were poor. The curriculum included tutoring by the undergraduate students, mentoring by members of the congregation, social skills/cultural conflict training (IMPPACT)[26] by church staff, and I conducted martial arts training.

Throughout the course, the university students engaged in conversations and weekly discussion groups about their growth, challenges, and goals as helpers, mentors, and learners. They engaged in self-reflection and program evaluation related to cultural emersion, multicultural helping, and educational strategies to effectively meet the needs of the elementary school students. Students also critically conversed on what they were learning in the community about meeting real needs among African American and Latino American male elementary school students. My favorite student assignment was the "Life and Helping Mission Portfolio," where students described the impact the course had on them. There were also positive changes in the church parishioners who served as "Community Elders." But the outcome that impacted me the most was the observation of one elementary school student in the program. At the closing family ceremony, this young man demonstrated his robotic arm to his parents. With pride, he used his remote to have the arm pick up a log and move it to another stack. I stood back and observed as his mother and father stood watching. Both parents were in tears. They later shared that they had never seen their son take that much interest in or focus on anything other than fighting. We also interviewed this young man's teacher at the close of the year. The teacher reported that this boy and many of the others in the after-school program had moved from the academic bottom of their classes to the middle or higher.

My hope is that, unlike the fictional Shawn Campbell in *Shots Fired*, the boys in the Brothers Energized Spirited Talented (BEST) Program will be able to resolve their conflicts and traumas around race, class, and gender. I do not know the long-term outcomes of the elementary students, but the undergraduate students reported that they gained a great deal from the course and were transformed by the opportunity to be vulnerable with their colleagues and the boys in the program. The course challenged our existing notions and standards about healing others. Several of the undergraduate students discussed how they learned to "be with" and accept the frustrations and actions of the young men as normal male behavior, rather than see them as troubled students. They learned that developing a relationship with the boys was critical to the boys becoming better students. The students realized the young men needed affirmation and validation rather than condemnation. This knowledge, according to students who have remained in contact with me, has enabled them to perform in their ministries without preconceived notions of good and bad behavior. Even though the students and church members were not professional counselors, they were very effective mentors and tutors because of the power of their relationships with the boys. The success of the BEST program is not surprising given its common components with effective counseling: models and techniques, counselors' skills, and counseling relationship.

Effective counseling and interventions with those recovering from trauma require excellent counseling knowledge and skills. Counselors must learn to adjust their internal biases and norms and change existing procedures to improve healing outcomes. That is, whether in a formal counseling setting, community intervention, or chaplaincy, the relationship between the participants remains a critically important factor, along with the experience of the counselor. As mental health providers counsel various socio-racial, ethnic, gender, and class groups, counselors will improve their effectiveness if they abandon hierarchies and internal biases against being vulnerable and available. We must face the fear of angering others and ostracizing neighbors. We must challenge practices that hinder relationships.

Counselors must engage in the relentless search for truth, justice, and equity. Mental health professionals cannot blame or shame people into being truth tellers. Rather, we must make true friends out of the enemies of healing—retraumatization and pathologizing. Clients in need of healing from racial trauma need counseling spaces where they are listened to and validated. Only then can counselors embrace the power of authenticity, push for victory and freedom, and openly engage in the struggle against racial trauma.

5

CULTURALLY APPROPRIATE COUNSELING

ONCE TRAUMA-INFORMED COUNSELORS acknowledge their internal biases, they are better positioned to effectively counsel traumatized ALANAs. The counselor can then create the counseling relationship where healing can occur. As mental health professionals strive to counsel from a more courageous therapy stance, they are equipped to openly combat racial traumas and engage issues of racial, gender, and class trauma.

Once counselors have honestly assessed their own posture, they can consider what counseling strategies would most help their clients. Trauma-informed therapy with ALANA clients can venture into the use of prayer, lament, bibliotherapy, mindfulness, or other grounding experiences as healing exercises. These techniques further the client's abilities to use the six senses in addition to their emotional reality.[1] These activities ground the client in their oppression tolerance and increase their pain tolerance. This act of grounding and tolerance increasing is particularly important if the client struggles with having a secure connection with their world and reality (dissociating).

Music has been an instrument of grounding for many trauma-informed counselors and clients. It bridges the space between the subjective and objective realities, allowing counseling to reach the "in-between space" between potentiality and authenticity.[2] Through music, the client can find an authentic and creative expression for their pain. Likewise, music therapy avails the client to personal and communal expressions of pain and sorrow, happiness and joy. Music can create new pathways between brain and body as we recall language through lyrics and promote healing through creative arts. A setting with music can create a safe space for trauma conversations and acti-vate the body to release and process traumatic events and relationships. Through music, counselors can transport clients to spaces where melo-dies, lyrics, and pictures promote healing.

As a counselor using DBT with traumatized and substance-abusing clients, I frequently used music as a component of mindful-ness training. We would listen to music that helped the client achieve emotional regulation, and I would dissuade clients from listening to music that triggered a traumatic state and negatively impacted their ability to regulate their emotions. When these clients would call in crisis situations, we would discuss exercises, music, and other emotion-regulating techniques for them to employ.

Other arts forms can be helpful in this process of grounding racially traumatized clients. The mandala is a very powerful grounding tool. Mandala coloring is a creative brain activity aimed at relieving tension and increasing focus. Having clients focus on coloring geometric shapes redirects them away from their distress. The word "mandala" means sacred circle. The circles of the mandala represent safe and contained spaces. Considered to be spiritually oriented, mandalas seek to engage the inner psychology of clients. Thus, mandalas have been found to be soothing and grounding for traumatized, and partic-ularly for racially traumatized, clients.

Poetry is another grounding activity counselors use with racially traumatized clients. It allows clients to distill emotions and find words to express difficult experiences. Often racially traumatized clients struggle to communicate their hurts in counseling. Writing or reading poetry opens a door to the clients' affect, which enables clients to give voice to their trauma, thereby providing the counselor access to important emotional materials. This avenue of communication can strengthen the mind, body, and soul connections of the client.

A powerful example of a poem a counselor could use in therapy with a racially traumatized African American client would be "Mr. Roosevelt Regrets" by Pauli Murray.[3] This poem juxtaposes the thesis that calls for national unity and peace against the antithesis of property violence and traumatizing behaviors that destroy freedom and mental health. Focusing on a poem such as this could be used to acknowledge the existence of mixed messages and painful experiences in the life of the ALANA individual and ALANA communities.

Even with all these steps and tools, therapy with racially traumatized clients is challenging. ALANAs enter counseling with experiences that have caused them emotionally debilitating agony. On their own, they are often unable to heal from their experiences and need professional assistance to recover and heal.

In addition to standard counseling techniques, embracing culturally specific aspects of the human interaction is an essential tool in our work with racially traumatized clients. The push for culturally based therapeutic treatment has received both positive and negative responses. For a time, most institutions (in government, education, the nonprofit arena) embraced this critical need due to the history and current experience of ALANAs in the United States. By addressing race-related realities honestly, America was once on a path to becoming a world leader in diversity, equity, and inclusion. Unfortunately, America is once again perceived internationally as a dangerous and racist society that is unable to come to terms with its past and present. Race and culturally specific treatments are being labeled unnecessary and judged ineffective by many. Powerful voices opposed to honoring and repairing the legacy of oppression for ALANAs are growing louder and receiving affirmation. As a result, culturally based treatment modalities for racial, gender, and class traumas are now characterized as divisive by some, and essential by others.

The perspective that racial and culturally based trauma counseling approaches are ineffective is an indication of an underlying misunderstanding, a misunderstanding of the intents of such interventions. Some mistakenly believe that ALANAs who have experienced racial, gender, and class traumas are not truly injured, or should get over themselves and move on. They are saying to racially traumatized

people, "We know you were hurt by systems of oppression; we realize
your lands were stolen and your properties were devalued, and we
acknowledge the unfair treatment you received, but that was then,
and this is now. Let's move on." Minimizing theories such as these are
divisive and disheartening. Counselors would do well to note that the
racially traumatizing experiences of oppression and disenfranchisement
among ALANAs already create a predisposition toward mistrusting
systems of power and privilege. The repudiation of the effects of racial,
gender, and class trauma on ALANAs further compounds the cultural
mistrust, which by proxy is often projected onto the counselor. This
suspicious attitude has resulted in low numbers of ALANAs seeking
and participating in mental health counseling. Already lacking access
to quality mental health counseling, ALANAs need counselors who
are aware, knowledgeable, and skilled at providing mental health
assistance.

For years the American Psychological Association has voiced
its concern regarding the lack of representation and participation of
ALANAs in mental health counseling.[4] Over and over, counseling
educators have called for the development of a pipeline model to
recruit and prepare ALANA counselors to work with ALANAs.
Undergirding this effort is the reality that, when appropriately
trained, persons who inherently understand the impact of oppression
on mental health are uniquely equipped to effectively counsel racially
traumatized clients. What is needed are persons trained and prepared
to create counseling spaces that are not only welcoming to ALANAs
but that are healing spaces. These counselors must be immunized
against hideous propositions of client-inherent inferiority, instead
looking for the unique strengths that ALANAs possess. Too many
counselors focus solely on the negative factors surrounding ALANAs.
They overlook the fact that racism, poverty, restricted opportunities,
and other destructive social variables coexist with protective factors
and positive influences. Through research, experiences, and relationships, a counselor trained in minority mental health is made aware of

the resilience of ALANAs. A counselor trained to combine scientific approaches with relationship-enhancing techniques is better suited to provide effective mental health treatment for them. A culturally sensitive counselor can draw out the problems from racially traumatized clients who typically withhold truth because they mistrust the culture, the system, and the counselor.[5]

To be effective, mental health professionals working with racially, gender, or economically traumatized clients must explore cultural (or systemic) mistrust in treatment without diagnosing the client as paranoid. Counselors must be willing to address the influence of the broader cultural context on both the counselor's own behavior and the behaviors of racial trauma clients. A mistrustful stance on the part of the client must be understood as reasonable, even logical, given the cultural and historical context. To fail to offer acceptance of cultural suspicions in counseling results in the counselor being perceived with even more suspicion. Once the counselor has been placed in the "suspicious box," there is little hope for an effective therapeutic relationship. And without the relationship, there is no apparatus to address the issues of racial trauma. When the client views the counselor with suspicion, the counselor is being grouped with every other oppressor in the client's world.

Along with not judging the client's cultural mistrust, a counselor must not make determinations about what qualifies as racial trauma. To battle over what is and what is not racially traumatizing for ALANA clients is futile; these arguments merely add to the client's pain. Who judges if a noose hanging over a door or an overheard racial slur about one's people is triggering? Clearly, it is not the responsibility of the counselor to judge if this matter or that matter causes a "legitimate" trauma response. What is imperative in these counseling situations is finding out from the client what specific acts, perpetrated on the client, triggered the trauma response and why those specific acts, at that specific time, produced the racial trauma. This knowledge is essential for the counseling to become a healing enterprise.

Focusing on the ALANA client's state of mind develops self-efficacy. This empirically validated best practice clearly deviates from counseling that devalues and deemphasizes in the name of challenging and correcting.[6]

By no means does affirming counseling seek to maintain the counseling relationship at the expense of confronting inaccurate impressions and avoiding truth. Rather, the goal is to create a hospitable healing relationship and environment where the racially traumatized ALANA client chooses to join with the counselor in a treatment process of comfort and discomfort.

Counseling centered on matters of trauma, race, gender, and class should focus on the recovery and effective treatment of the client. The goals for the counselor, then, are to identify the underlying sentiments that support the trauma and help the client respond to them in constructive ways. This counseling is victory-centered and client-directed. Counseling sessions can thoughtfully engage conversations on oppression, white supremacy, patriarchy, racism against Indigenous peoples, or anti-Asian sentiments. This approach cannot be summoned on demand, mandated, or prescribed. ALANAs are not a one-approach-fits-all group. Some ALANAs expect the counselor to assume a cultural perspective in counseling, while others prefer a standard treatment approach. What's critical is for the counselor to respond to the lived experiences of the client, not the perceived experiences of the counselor. Thus, mental health professionals who approach counseling as a collaboration with clients traumatized by racism and oppression in American society will develop a generative healing process as opposed to an inquisition-based approach that fosters mistrust.

For some counselors, culturally based therapy might seem unnecessary and not a good use of their time. In truth, effective counseling with racially traumatized clients requires a counselor to venture away from the norm. The counselor must enter the world of a person torn apart by class, gender, ethnicity, and/or race. This type of counseling is not easy; it is a big ask. It requires counselors to abandon their "pull yourself up by your bootstraps" mentality and enter the trauma and pain caused by oppression.

Even after practicing this type of prophetic liberating counseling for years, a counselor can still be baffled by the injuries caused by the traumas of racism, sexism, and classism. But quitting cannot be an option; in fact, quitting must become an abomination. For counselors committed to effective treatment of racially traumatized clients, faithful counseling is the only choice. It is said that the best predictor of future behavior is past behavior.[7] However, I have found this maxim to be inaccurate if there has been a cathartic experience. Mental health professionals working with racially traumatized clients must master the art of accessing the emotions of the client and reasoning with those emotions to promote psychological, social, and spiritual change.

Thus, effective counseling with racially traumatized clients requires that the counselor remove any blinders to the traumas of being avoided, ostracized, and discriminated against for reason of skin color, gender, or class. Competent trauma counselors bravely face the painful and overwhelming narratives of their ALANA clients. They boldly care-front the feelings of hostility and vulnerability that race-based physical and/or verbal assaults engender.[8] They navigate the discussions of generational violence and neglect as well as the retelling of traumatic events. These sensitized counselors avoid rescuing or defending the ALANA client from the pain, but rather seek to reconcile the client to the pain. This intimacy of authentic acceptance is life-giving. The counselor hears and attends to the suffering of the client. This counseling approach entails treating the anxiety and fear (trauma). This acceptance of race, gender, and class traumas transforms the pain of hopelessness into the hope of endurance.

When the traumas of race, gender, and class oppression are manifested in PTSD and CPTSD symptoms, they are more than faulty perceptions. These trauma symptoms occur because the traumatic memories are real. To nuance these complicated feelings, counselors must draw on their sense of vocation, realizing that they have been

fashioned to walk with ALANA clients through the valley of despair
and empowered to lead them to anxiety-controlled places. The client
must hear the invitation from the counselor to believe in the process
and trust that the counselor will accompany them down the path of
transformation. This process reminds me of encounters I had several
years ago with two young men in Haiti. I knew they dreamed of
leaving their mother country and accessing a better life in America.
The men wanted to experience lives more fruitful than the ones they
were experiencing in their Haitian orphanages and villages. My counseling was productive with them—but not because I offered a ticket
to a better life. The counseling was successful because we created safe
spaces to lament, explore, dream, and plan. These spaces enabled them
to mentally ascend their poverty. Our counseling allowed them to see
new possibilities and reframe their living as surviving and preparing for
future opportunities.

Creative awareness, knowledge, and skills in trauma-informed
counseling are extremely fruitful and revealing. Being creative using
the arts builds trust and allows the counselor to uncover acts and
trauma triggers that produced the racial trauma.

Counseling as Healing Art

Our world is bombarded with trauma-evoking events, from senseless acts of violence to natural disasters. These experiences are heart-
breaking, producing terror and devastation among those affected.
Many counseling professionals struggle to treat trauma, let alone
trauma entangled with issues of race. When the violence and tragedies are also race-based, the effects are compounded, confounding, and
recurrent. This point I know to be true, both from my professional and
personal experiences.

In 2008, a year after the mass shooting at Virginia Tech in
Blacksburg, Virginia, I was teaching an Introduction to Psychology
course at another Virginia university. Over three hundred college

students were enrolled in the course. I began class with my traditional blasting of the Red Hot Chili Peppers song, "Under the Bridge." Then, because of my training around the Virginia Tech shooting, I instituted an active shooter drill. The class and I practiced evacuating the lecture hall then reassembling once an all-clear was given. I recall stating to the class that I loved my life, but in an actual shooting, I was going to head in the direction of the shooter while they escaped. What I meant to convey by this statement is that even though I was just meeting my students, I cared about them. Later in the semester, I noticed a young student walking into class with a yoga mat. He and I chatted about yoga and martial arts, particularly how I used martial arts in my interventions with youth exhibiting behavioral problems. As the weeks progressed, we developed a friendly and respectful relationship as professor and student. After the semester ended, I was summoned by the university police to come to their station on campus. The officer notified me that the young man I befriended had voluntarily turned in a bookbag he carried daily to our psychology class—a bookbag containing a semi-automatic assault rifle and ammunition. As he surrendered his weapons, the student told the authorities that he had brought the weapon to class with the intention of killing everyone in the room, but he did not want to kill me because of our relationship, so he abandoned his own plan.

As I reflect on that experience, I am thankful that I did not typecast the student, who was Asian American and physically resembled the Virginia Tech shooter. Rather, I correctly suspected that the student was isolated and lonely. I am thankful for the spiritual and clinical inclinations that nudged me closer to him and to other individuals exhibiting these types of behaviors rather than withdrawing from them. In this case, that connection saved my life and the lives of my students.

In an insightful intervention by the Office of Student Affairs, the university created a plan for the student that consisted of probation, monitoring, and counseling. Because of my relationship with the young man and my position at the university, I was asked to counsel him, a task I accepted with humility.

I now realize the traumatic and socio-racial factors at play in our interactions. This Asian American student carried issues of trauma and race in his body and psyche. He was holding the collective trauma of his family's immigration and their racist interactions in their new country, encounters that included both microaggressions and outright racism. His outlook and perceptions of the world were colored by the experiences of racism he was taught to ignore. This student had not previously processed the legacy and trauma of immigration, assimilation, and adaptation. He shared that his anxiety was handed down from his parents. He disclosed that the legacy of immigration as an American of Asian descent had been tainted by harsh laws and immigration policies. As we talked, he shared that he had pushed out of consciousness and never discussed the traumas experienced by his family. As a result, he concluded that he moved through the world searching for belonging and acceptance, not previously found until he encountered an African American psychology professor.

The more our relationship of trust developed, the more he processed his trauma. He admitted that he had not made a connection between his traumatic racial experiences and his urge to hurt others and even end their lives. His mental capacities were overwhelmed by his experiences of rejection, pressure to be a model son, and desire to be a respectable citizen. This young man did not embrace his family's life narrative. He knew that the glorified "being-an-Asian-in-America story" did not sync with his reality. As an American immigrant, he felt like an invader and an outsider. As an Asian American, he felt invisible. The result was a young man at odds with his family's narrative and a US citizen who felt emotional pain in his body that needed a way out. His unconscious and repressed pain manifested as a senseless urge to replicate the Virginia Tech shooting and force people to acknowledge him. In such situations, only an authentic relationship provides the connection required to change course—to foster resilience and promote healing. The prospect of such growth empowered this young man to move beyond our professor–student relationship to a therapeutic space where he could process his pain.

In our safe space, the student discussed his rage at high school classmates and a school community that, he felt and experienced, had never invited him to belong. He was confounded by family and friends who he perceived as oblivious to his trauma. Wanting them to notice and acknowledge his pain, he believed that the mass shooting would cause them to pay his personhood some attention. Fortunately, he never took the opportunity to express his rage in class. Instead, he was able to redirect his feelings of isolation away from thoughts of dying to thoughts of living. By taking his book bag of weapons to the campus police, he broke the vicious circle of despair.

Once he and I processed what led him to this point, we focused on reducing his anxiety and anger. I introduced the fact that I, too, was angry and frustrated as a young man growing up in a segregated Detroit. I told him about my complicated relationship with my father and my father's abandonment of our family because of his PTSD. When he asked how I got over my anger, I shared the origins of my name and the biblical verse that accompanies it, Micah 6:8. We discussed how the experiences with my father and the focus on my name taught me that the goal of my life was to act justly, love mercy, and walk humbly with our God. I reviewed that my name being different from my father allowed me to develop an identity separate from him (individuation). I shared that I sought and found support and encouragement from my church pastor and other community leaders.

My intervention with this young man was tailored around the blueprint of transformation: releasing, lamenting, reflecting, waiting, and acting, the approach tailored to racial trauma work with ALANAs. First, we discussed the process of humility (releasing) as we empty ourselves of our pain and our glory—for the sake of our loved ones. We discussed how I joined an African American fraternity on my college campus and developed connections with my fraternity brothers

that allowed me to connect with ancestorial members like Thurgood
Marshal and Martin Luther King Jr. I shared that this humbling experience placed my pain and trauma in relation to my dreams of leading
my people. We then focused on him letting go and transforming his
hurt and pain into his dreams of freedom.

Next, we focused on lamenting and enduring our suffering. This
work centered around the metaphor of traveling through dangerous
valleys, helping him notice the water and grass in the valley pastures,
gifts to aid his survival. Throughout the counseling we used poetry and
art to examine his suffering and teach him to trust that his emptying
had prepared him to endure the pain before letting go of that pain.

One counseling goal was to teach the young man to see the
upside of suffering (reflecting). Given our common interest in physical
training, we discussed the pain and struggle in mastering the martial
arts. We could celebrate the learning that occurs when we used reflection to endure training hardships.

Then we moved to conversations and exercises around waiting.
Our conversations revolved around situations where the young man
and his family benefited from voluntarily surrendering to the isolation and rejection he felt as an Asian American. We noted the success
the family experienced in business and the generational wealth they
were able to accrue. We revisited the upside of the racially related
suffering he experienced and used this knowledge of his racial struggles
to support the notion of releasing, lamenting, reflecting, and waiting
while suffering.

We paired this cognitive learning with the psychological techniques of muscle relaxation and systematic desensitization around his
racial trauma. Together we developed a stress hierarchy around the
concept of living in the space around his stress. The muscle relaxation
and stress hierarchy helped the client access the space between stimulus
and response.[9] The young man and I labeled this stage of counseling as
sacred space, focusing on his living in the tension of what he saw, felt,

and wanted. In this space we oscillated between contemplation and analysis. We recognized his waiting all semester to turn his backpack in to campus police as a strength he possessed—the strength to wait—not to wait passively, but to wait for restoration, restructuring, renewal.

Our final focus of counseling was on restoration via problem solving—consciously acting to positively remedy his problems. During this phase, we used my faith-related acronym, IMPPACT: I Must Pause Pray Analyze Chill and Take Action.[10] IMPPACT includes a seven-step problem-solving model: I Must (ownership), Pause and Pray (self-imposed time out), Analyze (problem solving), Chill (waiting), and Take Action (executing the decision). We focused on the quality of his actions as a final step toward overcoming his frustrations.

As we considered action steps, we kept in mind another major goal of our work together: to reduce the anxiety of the student around his perceived loss of power and relational isolation. In many ways, counseling around traumatic racial experiences is about the abuse of power and absence of love. Like this student, many ALANAs experience being violated and terrified by acts intended to control and conquer them. In turn, they often repress memories of the oppression. Unfortunately, these feelings are often repressed and felt physiologically in the body, where they continue to unconsciously affect the psycho-social-spiritual functioning of the victim. This maladaptive behavior is particularly true and relevant when working with racially traumatized clients. Counseling to remedy these ills can focus on anchoring or reanchoring the client. In this regard, techniques centered on establishing radical self-responsibility and communal covenants can facilitate healing.

The concept of radical self-responsibility was helpful in our work together. We defined radical self-responsibility as a mindset of being answerable, responsible, and accountable to his own power and control. The young man used I-statements to gain a sense of control over his life. I-statements typically focus on what the client thinks, feels, needs, and would like. Articulating these thoughts and feelings is often challenging but is so important. My young client and I worked through the following exercise: "When you _____, I feel _____ because _____. In the future I would like _____." In this exercise, the client might say, "When you see me only as a model minority, I feel devalued and useless because I am more than my physical appearance. In the future, please see me for who I really am."

This work of taking radical responsibility included focusing the student on living a balanced life, one that took care of his mind, body, and soul. We discussed his maintaining a healthy diet, getting at least seven hours of sleep every night, exercising, and reengaging in meditation. Our work centered on his being honest with himself and addressing the lies he believed about himself. We did a lot of cognitive work around his negative self-talk and his inability to accept his imperfections. This training involved his heart-muscle, an area as important as his physical muscles.

Articulating a communal covenant was a technique used with this young man to focus him on covenantal rather than individual relationships. A communal covenant is a binding promise that makes clear the commitments for communion.[11] It seeks to establish a sense of community and safety, and code of conduct. This intervention was used as an attempt to challenge his worldview and cultural way of thinking about relationships. Many professional counselors avoid working with ideas such as communal covenants; however, when a client has experienced betrayal and distrust in a system, this is a technique that remedies the ill. This young man and I acknowledged the impact of our accepting and supportive relationship, using it as the foundation for the communal covenant he created.

Clinical work with racial trauma clients is heart-work. This type of counseling must address the emotional quagmire that results from racial oppression persistent over generations. Too often counselors want to move quickly through issues of race and pass by the racial abuse, neglect, disenfranchisement, and violence experienced by ALANAs. It is tempting for counselors to focus on the outward symptoms of anxiety and fear, particularly when physical symptoms (racing heart, insomnia, shallow breathing, clammy hands, head-aches, and muscle aches) are the presenting problems. But addressing the internal emotions of doubt, worry, fight, flight, or freeze is very important when working with racially traumatized clients.

One technique to address the fight-flight-freeze propensities of ALANAs is the mirroring technique. By consciously using active listening and reflecting the client's affect and body language, the coun-selor can access and reason with the emotional self of the client and further develop the therapeutic alliance.[12] It is a very simple technique that is rarely or poorly used by counselors but, when correctly done, mirroring simultaneously communicates the hope and trust as well as the doubt and despair of the counseling relationship. Mirroring allows counseling to occur in a manner that promotes unconditional posi-tive regard toward racially traumatized clients. This approach contrasts with a culture that denies or minimizes racist microaggressions expe-rienced by many ALANA clients. Relational/spiritual mirroring is a technique that offers clients acceptance and warmth in a seemingly rejecting and callous world.

Correct use of the mirroring technique conveys the meaning of *sawabona*—"I see you." During our sessions we used yoga poses and martial arts as mirroring techniques. I would ask the student to display his pain in a stance or pose, and I would mirror his technique, communicating the emotions that he was experiencing. We laughed and corrected one another's techniques, a lightness that led to bonding. The joy of mutually kicking, holding stances, moving, and falling was a life-changing delight.

Several years after our counseling work together, I encountered the young man working as a cook at a local restaurant. He had stopped out of school for a time.[13] Though still dealing with mental health issues, he was connecting with people. He shared that he was thankful to have met me and felt that I had saved his life through the relation-ship I had with him as a professor and a counselor. When counselors

compassionately address racial trauma, they can make a positive difference in the lives of their clients.

Counseling as Relational Reconciliation

As experienced in the counseling with this young student, counseling
amid cultural mistrust is a practice of reconciliation. The counselor
serves as an ambassador of reconciliation, a critical and exciting
aspect of counseling. A counselor focused on reconciliation witnesses
suffering and sees the world through the lens of lament. This is an
honorable position, one that involves empathy, recovery, healing, and
renewal. Counseling is an invitation from our clients to join them in a
work of internal and external relationship restoration.

Reconciliation is the antithesis of denial. To deny the pain and
problems caused by clients' experiencing racial trauma is to engage
in politically based clinical paralysis. Conversely, counselors who view
counseling with racially traumatized clients as a work of relational
reconciliation counsel from the heart and move easily to deep introspection and redemption. Viewing counseling as relational reconciliation empowers the counselor to caringly confront the realities of racial
wrongdoing and explore with the client the manners in which racial,
gender, and class oppression have perpetrated trauma.

Relational reconciliation draws the psychological defenses of the
client into the counseling conversations. Because the counseling has
shifted to focus on the restoration of the internal and external brokenness, it embraces the possibility of transformation and avoids the
temptation of cheap grace. In order to truly reconcile, ALANA clients
must detoxify their systems from the poison of race trauma.[14] Given
that our world remains troubled by philosophies of racial superiority,
aristocracy, and terrorism, counselors cannot escape the call to serve as
justly acting reconcilers with their ALANA clients.

To be fully committed to reconciling relationships is a call to
engage in the uplift of all humanity. It is a summons to be our best
selves. As mental health professionals, we realize that we cannot alleviate

all our clients' intrapersonal and interpersonal conflicts. However, we can engage the clinical narratives of our clients as reconciliation doorways. Counselors of traumatized ALANAs must accept at face value the damaged people who present with urgent need of healing, and mental health professionals must avoid comparing client narratives to their own life stories or those of other clients. A life of discomfort and struggle for one person might develop resilience, but a similar challenge for another client might result in unresolved difficulty. Again, the question for the mental health professional is how to help alleviate the suffering. Counselors must focus on how clinical interactions can be used to facilitate intrapersonal and/or interpersonal reconciliation.

For counselors to effectively respond to this call to be relational reconcilers, we require a blueprint for personal and clinical transformation. This transformation blueprint was used with the ALANA student who brought a weapon to class and, as the case illustration shows, involves accompanying and directing individuals through a process of clinical exploration around five interpersonal and intrapersonal dynamics mentioned earlier in this chapter: releasing, lamenting, reflecting, waiting, and acting.

To elaborate on the blueprint, we must first learn to empty ourselves of life-crippling mental and physical burdens. To many ALANAs, letting go of the injuring experiences is challenging. Often racially traumatized clients hold on to their oppression as the most important experience of their lives and cannot envision life without it. Counselors can help clients imagine that emptying oneself of pain is an empowering gift of freedom and reorientation. This release from the emotional captivity of traumatic experiences equips the ALANA client to battle the imprisoning powers of oppression. Once the client cognitively realizes that they can release the hold of oppression, the client can counter the tendency to deploy the fight, flight, or freeze anxiety pattern. When the power of negative emotions is diminished, the connection between oppression and interpersonal and intrapersonal anxiety can be severed. This paradoxical intervention is imperative because frequently clients cannot embrace the pain of oppression until some measure of relief is obtained. Emotional release provides emotional relief.

After the release stage, counselors are then positioned to assist the client with the second interpersonal and intrapersonal dynamic, lamenting loss. Frequently, trauma-work healing is derailed because the client never engages in mourning what was lost. Learning to frame feelings of regret, disappointment, and sadness is an important objective in the healing process, and a counselor can use poetry, music, or visual art to examine suffering from a bit of a distance. Through lament materials and lament rituals, the client develops healing metaphors and identifies the positives of suffering. This form of creative arts therapy will help the client during the healing process.

Reflecting is the next component in this blueprint of reconciliation. As mentioned in Chapter 1, reflecting occurs in the mental, emotional, and physical space between the stimulus (oppression) and the response (trauma).[15] This space becomes healing space when the racially traumatized client contemplates the imposition, surrender, sacrifice, and denial that has been endured. Reflecting through meditation, reading, talking, and/or writing creates room to contemplate the gains and losses of enduring oppression.

Waiting is another important component of this transformation process. As counselors we learn alongside our racially traumatized ALANA clients, trusting that the process of releasing, lamenting, and reflecting will lead to effective waiting. Trauma can halt emotional development, and anxiety produces unease around past, present, and future life events. Learning to wait teaches a traumatized client not to act prematurely. As the counselor and client spend time waiting, they learn to breathe and to believe again. Waiting is learning to be patient during a crisis. Waiting is preparing to stand with a new awareness once the healing path materializes. Waiting is holding the suffering of life until transformation is achieved.

Finally, we must assist our traumatized ALANA clients to act with power. The goal is for clients to apply problem-solving techniques to remedy their traumatic situations. One of the key principles of mental health counseling is that problem solving enables the client to identify challenges to overcome in the future as well as strengths and opportunities. Whereas trauma experiences remove the possibility of making choices, solving problems returns the power of making choices to the client. Counselors can use visualization, acronyms, and other techniques as effective strategies for solving problems.

This model of transformation allows counselors to avoid the trap of asking questions only about what has happened and what has been broken. A focus on transformation and reconciliation creates space for imagining existence in a nonoppressive world and a life-generating social system. This is visionary work—work resistant to fixing the pain, but rather living in the ambiguity and liminality of life as a recovering racially traumatized person. Obtaining transformation is to find a sanctuary for the racial trauma. This process moves beyond controlling, fixing, or clarifying the brokenness. Transformation is the ability to stay where the suffering is while gaining the wisdom to live comfortably in your reality. In this reality, the oppression does not produce trauma. Rather, this transformed existence creates a haven from internal and external oppressive ideologies and actions because the client is empowered to walk as a healed person, even during oppression.

In this counseling work of transformation, suffering signals the need to create a space for renewal. From this perspective, counseling becomes a transitional space that serves to mediate the client's inner reality with the shared reality of living as a racial minority, woman, or under-resourced disenfranchised individual.[16] This transitional space negotiates the tension between the traumatized individual and the environment where the trauma occurred, and this reconciliation-based counseling helps the client integrate the mind, body, and soul with the uncertainty of living in a complicated world. Such work addresses the dissociation response that a traumatized client typically uses to manage the triggering and activation that occurs when the body feels unsafe.

The racially traumatized client lives in a body that unconsciously and intuitively connects the current situation with past harmful situations. A reconciliation approach acknowledges that the client has been in situations where power was used to control and abuse them. Before healing, the representations of the traumatizer are always with the traumatized. By working for reconciliation, the traumatized client learns to trust in the counseling process of enduring hardship and growing from suffering.

Connecting in the counseling process prepares both the counselor and the client for the challenging journey. This process positions the counselor to watch for trauma responses in clients. These trauma responses indicate that the client cannot tolerate the triggering of traumatic memories, and transformation-focused reconciliation counseling helps the client integrate the trauma into their whole self. This work is challenging but important. By helping a client tolerate the discomfort and painful memories of trauma, we are helping them to reconcile. This process is what trauma-informed counseling names "repairing the insecure attachment." The toxic and antagonistic societal zeitgeist toward ALANAs is reconciled with the faith that releasing, lamenting, reflecting, waiting, and acting on the traumatic materials builds resilience and fortitude. Counseling with a healthy, reconciled counselor or trauma-informed counselor holds the best opportunity for the client to coalesce the traumatic experiences and overcome the resulting disorientation.

The process of aiding the client to coalesce and overcome the feelings, notions, and experiences of oppression leads to a freedom from isolation that elevates. This phenomenon of sitting in counseling with a racially traumatized client and helping them arrive at a place of tranquility where they do not feel alone and no longer feel responsible for their abuse is electrifying. Though evidence-based practice is incorporated, this type of counseling not only uses art, it is art. This approach to racial trauma embraces complex human emotions and strives for healing.

6

CLINICAL CREATIVITY

CREATIVITY IS ART, and some say that art resembles life. In the Marvel Disney+ television series *Moon Knight*, we find a fictional display of the effects of trauma on one's personality. In episode 5, it is revealed that Marc and Steven are the dissociated personalities of the superhero Moon Knight. The personalities have been in a fight to the death with the show's villain, Dr. Harrow, and are now in an emotional purgatory or dream state. The purgatory is an asylum, and the personalities of the Moon Knight are being treated by Dr. Harrow. Marc and Steven must confront their shared traumatic memories to leave the asylum.

During counseling, Dr. Harrow shares with Marc that the integration work he is doing is difficult and painful. The doctor tells Marc that he must now peer deeper into the painful moments that created him. After hours of work, the doctor asks Marc two very insightful questions: "Did you create Steven to help you hide from all the awful things you have done in your life? Or did Steven create you to punish the world for what your mother did to him?"

Dr. Harrow then tells Marc that there is only one way for him to find the answer: Marc will have to share his painful memories with his dissociated personality (Steven). The doctor tells Marc that there can never be progress without understanding. The episode then has both personalities view the past incident where Marc is severely beaten by his grieving mother, after which he dissociates for the first time to survive the trauma of the beating and the anger of his mother. The episode then skips to when Marc returns for his mother's wake but is unable to participate. His dissociated self (Steven) watches as Marc cannot say goodbye to his mother, breaks down in the street, and retreats into a semi-permanent Steven personality.

After showing the viewers the traumatic events and the pitiful response, the two personalities watch Marc's memory of his mother's wake. Steven (the created personality) tells Marc (the traumatized personality) that his younger brother's accidental death was not his fault. Steven caringly shares with Marc that he was just a child when his brother drowned; there was nothing he could do. This is a clear example of a healing moment for a traumatized personality.

Trauma therapy with racially traumatized clients may or may not progress as linearly as the counseling dramatization in *Moon Knight*. Additionally, mental health professionals may not be able to effectively orchestrate intense conversations between or around the internal "personalities" of our trauma clients. Nevertheless, the procedures and principles illustrated in the episode—such as exploring how trauma experiences affect thinking, processing the traumatic experiences' impact on the mind, body, and spirit, and finding meaning and purpose in community and relationships—demonstrate effective approaches to trauma-informed therapy.

The *Moon Knight* episode is an apt illustration for counselors working with racially traumatized ALANA clients. The Moon Knight suffered from racial and gender trauma, developing a dissociated personality to cope with his trauma. W. E. B. Du Bois addressed this phenomenon of dissociating, which he labeled double consciousness.[1] Du Bois saw that a negative consequence of the double consciousness was a negative view of the self through the eyes of another and the measurement of one's worth through the treatment of oppression. Dr. Dubois spoke of the Black American as having "two souls, two bodies, two thoughts, two unreconciled strivings."[2] But Du Bois also saw the potentiality to develop a psychological defense from this double consciousness. He visualized a path forward where Black Americans would marry the two selves "into a better and truer oneself."[3]

This reassociation is the hard work of trauma-informed counseling. Developing this type of insight into and out of traumatic experiences is the gift and art of reframing. To nurture the traumatic experiences of rejection and oppression and then turn them into a powerful second sight is to develop a superpower. Developing this superpower in the racially traumatized client is an important counseling task. It occurs when the counselor focuses on the resiliency and adaptability of ALANAs, and is made possible when the counselor helps the client realize the complexities of their situation and uses counseling to celebrate the client's survival and desire to be whole and healthy. The dynamics of clinical effective practices empower the client to rise above low expectations and systemic disadvantages.[4]

The *Moon Knight* episode shows that complicated cases of trauma-informed counseling require probing questions to open a client for transformation. We can try to reframe painful events and paint them with flowery colors, but this camouflage only avoids the necessary work and prolongs the client's suffering. We must confront the elephant sitting comfortably in our counseling spaces. We must ask the uncomfortable but pertinent questions. We must refuse to be co-conspirators with clients who are risk avoidant and pain intolerant. We must walk the perilous, less-traveled path of culturally appropriate trauma-informed counseling.

Road Map to Healing Trauma Wounds

To travel the difficult and hidden path of trauma-informed counseling with ALANA clients, we need an excellent road map. Our map must consist of counseling strategies that are clear and centered around the problems to be solved. It must engage ALANA clients who have been negatively affected by racial, gender, and class oppression.

Interestingly, maps are designed to prevent the traveler from getting lost, but skillfully engaging loss is an essential aspect of the counseling map. And those who have been lost themselves can turn out to be the best guides. Counselors who have faced a major tragedy like the death of a friend, child, or spouse (or have personally dealt with an important loss like a marriage, career, or sibling) have been provided with a clinical acumen that will guide them through the emotionally charged boulevards of trauma-informed counseling with ALANA clients. Resolved experiences with disaster and loss can furnish a counselor with the proficiencies to venture into a client's faulty places—the emotional circumstances in which clients are experiencing anguish and unreasonableness. A counselor who has experienced and survived life's ordeals frequently possesses the disposition to facilitate meaning-making out of seemingly futile situations.

This is not to say that a counselor who has not learned to survive and thrive from loss is ill-equipped to work with ALANA trauma clients. What I am claiming is that the counselor who has learned from loss and disaster may be predisposed to creating healing spaces for racially traumatized ALANA clients. A prime example of a counselor whose personal tragedy provided a road map to a healing program is Robert Fazio, PhD. Rob was a doctoral student in the counseling psychology program that I taught in when the New York City Twin Towers were attacked on September 11, 2001. When I learned of the attack, I immediately thought of Rob's father, who worked there. I had met Ronald C. Fazio Sr. just weeks before, during his visit to our campus in August. Shortly after the attack I learned that Robert Fazio's father died in the South Tower on 9-11. But the stories of his bravery and courage are legendary.

Many survivors shared stories of how they remembered Mr. Fazio exiting the building safely. Once he was outside and looked up at the South Tower, he realized the grave danger those inside the building were in and the need for employees to evacuate immediately. Realizing the urgency, Mr. Fazio went back inside the building and led many others out, holding the door open for their safe exit. Tragically and bravely Mr. Fazio died holding the door as the South Tower collapsed.

Even with the accounts of Mr. Fazio's heroics, the death of this man was devastating for his family. But Dr. Rob Fazio channeled the loss of his father into a program titled Hold the Door for Others (HTD). Rob rallied family, friends, and colleagues like me to join him in creating a healing community centered on post-traumatic growth.

Guided by Rob's leadership, professionals, family, friends, and volunteers have gathered annually for over twenty years in New Jersey and New York to help others grow through their losses, just as Rob and I have. We have redefined how people framed their grief and focused our clinical skills on assisting others to grow through their traumas and losses.

Dr. Fazio and the HTD team have developed numerous resources to help people navigate through sudden loss and the accompanying anxiety. One theoretical component that I have found particularly useful in my work is the Optimism/Hope, True-Meaning, Humor, Emotional Intelligence, Resilience, Spirituality, and Self-Confidence (OTHERS(S)) model (see Figure 6.1).

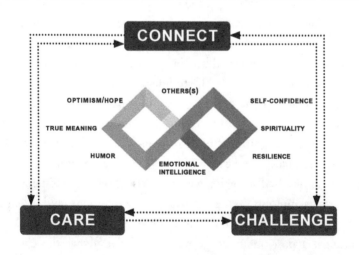

Figure 6.1. The OTHERS(S) model: Optimism/Hope, True-Meaning, Humor, Emotional Intelligence, Resilience, Spirituality, and Self-Confidence (OTHERS(S)) model. Source: adapted from R. J. Fazio and L. M. Fazio, eds., *Finding Your Way through Sudden Loss and Adversity* (Closter, NJ: Hold the Door for Others, 2006), https://holdthedoor.com/wp-content/uploads/2018/06/finding-your-way.pdf.

It has been an honor to work with HTD to help broken individuals and communities find resources as they strive for closure and release. The OTHERS(S) model is a best-practice intervention that reaches into the community to engage and heal. It provides a map to healing based on a family and nation's loss. It was developed and refined by mental health professionals working with trauma clients and has been used in counseling practices with racially traumatized ALANA clients.[5] The OTHERS(S) model was not specifically developed to treat clients suffering from racial trauma; however, it is a prime example of a program that could be adapted to this population because it successfully creates a healing space for those suffering from loss. For example, it has been gratifying to discuss the optimism/hope that many ALANA clients feel when they have worked to reconcile their anger at the system and mistreatment they have experienced.

The model is robust and allows space to discuss resilience and self-confidence. This has assisted us in our work with ALANA women whose experiences with race and gender oppression left them battered and broken. Using hope and humor, the model prepares these women to face their oppressors with self-confidence, realizing they are resilient. Using a post-traumatic growth orientation has aided us at HTD in our work with other ALANA clients. Specifically, we have been able to help them recognize the areas of emotional intelligence that they excel at and areas where they need to grow. In responding to clients' racially traumatized struggles, we have assisted them in reducing their depressive symptoms, better managing their emotions, and soliciting help from their families and communities. In addition to managing emotions, a post-traumatic growth perspective allows the client to consider helping their families and communities as they struggle to overcome broader racial trauma. As the counseling focus shifts from the individual to the family and community, the concepts, principles, and strategies of restorative justice are also profitable for counseling racially traumatized ALANA clients.

Restorative justice is an adaptable and meaningful theoretical paradigm focused on the brokenness and racial trauma within the US justice system.[6] A restorative justice framework focuses on the creation and maintenance of healing relationships between perpetrators and victims through sharing personal narratives—this is justice that reconciles and transforms broken relationships and disrupted communities, and that focuses on healing, not punishment. Growing out of the civil rights and Black Power movements of the 1960s, the approach brings balance to racial trauma interventions. This balance is possible because of the dialectical embrace of the warrior–healer archetype. Engaging the tension between perpetrator and victim creates space to help clients investigate the dilemma between being acted upon and being the actor. Too frequently traumatized clients are trapped, consciously or unconsciously, in the victim–oppressor tragedy. A restorative justice approach requires communication around the costs and losses of turning anger into forgiveness and remorse into acceptance.

Many conceptualize restorative justice as a praxis simply focused on disrupting the school-to-prison pipeline and interrupting mass incarceration. Those are important components of restorative justice work; however, in addition to disrupting the social harms of incarceration, restorative justice also serves as a relational, proactive prevention and intervention strategy. It can be used to connect or reconnect the racially traumatized ALANA client's internal self to the losses and to reveal unidentified strengths. Restorative justice theory can further reconcile the individual client to the external community, community principles, and community wisdom.

In short, this is a labor to alter worldviews. For some of us this is a labor of love, for others a labor of necessity. To facilitate a racially traumatized ALANA client in transforming their victim-based worldview into a victor-based worldview is a rewarding experience. Helping a client recognize that they wear a mask of oppression and what that mask means, then watch them cognitively and behaviorally remove the mask is exhilarating.

As discussed in Chapter 2, the mask is the false self, and to unmask is to find the true self. Additionally, the mask of oppression is a shame-prone, performance-based, protective shield worn to cover oneself and hide from oppression. Whereas the mask is worn out of an overreliance on the self, the restorative justice approach is fruitful in the work of mask removal because it focuses on community. Mask removal is a liberation act and entails naming your pain and finding ways to heal. It requires developing the desire to recover and finding internal and external spaces in which to do the hard work of reconstruction and renewal.

In my work with racially traumatized ALANA clients, I have used the Peacemaker–Healer–Warrior–Hero paradigm to creatively work to remove masks of oppression (see Figure 6.2). In my clinical work I have found that most clients are socialized to play one of the roles, and the roles often conflict with their sense of self. The model is used to illustrate and alleviate the conflicts that result from striving to fulfill or survive social rules, edicts, and oppressive practices.

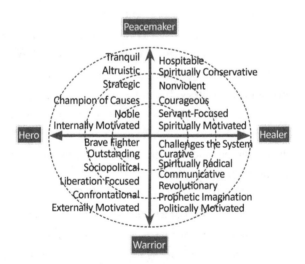

Figure 6.2. McCreary's Peacemaker–Healer–Warrior–Hero paradigm. Source: developed by Micah McCreary, this paradigm is a conceptual model based on clinical experience and theory.

As the name indicates, the Peacemaker is an individual involved in peacemaking, typically helping the family and the system avoid conflict, violence, and altercations. The Peacemaker is a person free from disturbances. Peacemakers are typically very spiritual and are very likely to engage in processes that generate peace, such as negotiations and arbitration.

The Healer in the model is the co-therapist or the doctor in the system. Healers typically have the talents of vision, intervening, and channeling. Healers are often charismatic leaders, shamans, and medicine men. The Healer is focused on curing, problem solving, and/or preventing injury.

The Warrior archetype is thought of as the brave and experienced fighter. They are the provider and protector of psychological, spiritual, emotional, and financial matters. The Warrior assesses threat and danger to the wellbeing of the community and provides provision and protection.

Finally, in the Peacemaker–Healer–Warrior–Hero paradigm, the Hero is the person with courage, outstanding achievements, and noble qualities. The Hero is conceptualized as the crusader, rescuer, soldier, winner, and team player.

Using the Peacemaker–Healer–Warrior–Hero paradigm, a counselor can explore the mask worn by the client for propensities to clothe the psyche in the false vestiges of oppression. We look for markers of shame, guilt, and oppressive acts. We examine the internalization of lies and false assumptions that shaped the client's reality. We ask clients to visualize where they would be on the diagram if they removed the mask of oppression. We then develop a treatment plan for increasing the behaviors and characteristics of the chosen Peacemaker–Healer–Warrior–Hero trait or traits. Specifically, we watch movies, read novels, and discuss the clients' reactions to various protagonists and characters. We then explore their thoughts, feelings, and impressions of the characters and relate these conversations back to the client's mask-wearing. The goal is to shift the connection from the mask of oppression and trauma to an identity of health, hope, and freedom.

So, if the client and I were to watch *Moon Knight*, we would begin with a discussion of how the Moon Knight, Marc, and Steven each wear a mask of oppression. Using probing questions, we would discuss the character the client strongly identifies with based on negative (or oppressive) qualities. Then, we would focus on how the role is against the client's core self. Finally, we would discuss ways that the identified role is a mask and work to shift the client to embrace an identity of hope. In the case of the Moon Knight, the work would include integrating the hero personality (Marc) with the peaceful personality (Steven).

Using the Peacemaker–Healer–Warrior–Hero paradigm in counseling with racially traumatized ALANA clients helps the client to identify the natural impact of oppressive stressors on their personality and behaviors. It also aids the counselor to clarify the consequences of the racial, gender, and class stressors on the client. During this work, it is important that the counselor and client retain the knowledge about the impact of the trauma in the process of masking (or in the case of the Moon Knight, dissociating). This information is critical for relapse prevention and thus must be included in the client's trauma treatment roadmap.

Post-trauma growth and restorative justice theories are useful in tending to the trauma wounds of ALANA clients. They both promote self-knowledge and personal responsibility. Self-knowledge is basically an awareness of oneself as an individual. It is an indispensable trait for recovery and healing and is the opposite of being unaware and unconscious of one's feelings, emotions, and motivations. Without self-knowledge, change is difficult or near impossible, particularly as it relates to trauma-injured clients, so increasing levels of self-knowledge is an important goal when counseling racially traumatized clients. ALANA clients have been instructed through laws, behaviors, media, and social conditions that they are not people of value, that their feelings and thoughts don't matter. The inner dynamics that result from these negative communications and experiences must be processed.

The constant rejection and unwillingness of society to affirm the humanity of ALANA persons results in many negative outcomes that affect individuals and communities. Counselors working with ALANA clients oppressed because of their race, gender, or class must intentionally address and care-front the inner dynamics that require transformation. This acknowledgment and attention to the brokenness is a direct showdown with any unconscious and unresolved issues of low self-esteem, guilt, and shame. Coming face to face with our weakness, in a caring and safe environment, weakens the bonds of oppression. Confessing the brokenness (fear, betrayal, hopelessness) creates a space to cultivate self-awareness relative to personal and corporate negative behaviors. Growing in self-knowledge is critical to restoring community and rectifying negative patterns.

Self-knowledge also buffers the client against internal and external threat narratives. Living as an ALANA individual in the United States is to live under the constant threat of hurt, harm, and danger. To live without privilege and status is a vulnerable position, but to live in a community that threatens your existence when you already feel powerless is unbearable. This vulnerability, produced by the assumptions of inferiority, further necessitates the counselor working to increase the traumatized client's self-knowledge. To live as an ALANA person in the United States is also to exist in a world where your being is either ignored or perceived unimportant. To accept this external classification is to live as a subhuman with the internal and external conflicts that categorization creates. Internally, ALANAs often vacillate between feelings of despair and relief, anger and excitement, depression and elation, and rejection and acceptance. The positions and labels imposed on them by society have a profound impact on their internal definitions and conversations. Externally, ALANAs are represented and perceived as criminal, deviant, and emotionally immature. This typecasting has a tremendous negative toll on the individual and collective self-esteem of ALANAs and results in all sorts of emotional complications. As ALANAs work internally and externally to combat these oppressive acts, increasing positive self-knowledge is a protective intervention.

One strategy to increase positive self-knowledge is assisting a traumatized ALANA client to work and advocate in their community for human rights and human dignity. Advocacy work is hard work but it can focus the self away from one's own difficulties by concentrating on the difficulties of others; healing can come when a hurt person helps another. Time and time again, I have observed an ALANA family accept a community member from outside their family system into their home. This action was based on memory of the host being rejected and they were not going to reject another. I will never forget when I asked my nuclear family if we could take in a young man in our community who was struggling during his mother's incarceration. Without hesitation the answer was, "Of course!"

ALANAs are relational beings, formed by their intrapersonal and interpersonal social experiences and contexts, and the joy of therapy is helping humans re-create themselves within the stresses and pressures of life. This re-creation is accomplished through retrieving and reworking their internal and external narratives. Our stories are the constructs that constitute our very being, and a trauma-informed counselor who helps an ALANA client generate healing stories that are based on self-knowledge and self-awareness heals the brokenness and lifts them above the chaos. This work also prevents further harm to the psyche and violence against the self. Self-knowledge is a step toward empowering the client to live and feel fully human.

Having self-knowledge and being self-aware is difficult; these are skills to be developed, and I have spoken to or counseled numerous individuals who were clueless about their roles and contributions to many things, from job conflicts to church squabbles. Counselors, even more than clients, must develop certain awareness and self-knowledge competencies to work effectively with trauma victims. Counselors must be able to appreciate and understand the impact of trauma on wellbeing; tailor intervention to honor race, ethnicity, culture, and diversity; adapt to various family systems and family dynamics; intervene around development issues and ableism; and incorporate strategies around strengths, resilience, and growth. As seen in *Moon Knight's* Marc character, self-knowledge is often suppressed when a client experiences complex trauma. Marc compartmentalized his painful feelings and memories, dissociating and detaching himself from his emotions and awareness of self. His character represented a client disconnected from thoughts, feelings, and bodily sensations, a person operating behaviorally without conscious awareness. The response of the counselor, Dr. Hallow in Marc's case, was to inquire about the behavior. In actual practice, the counselor must also affirm and engage the disconnection, lack of awareness, and unconscious behavior. The counselor must seek to stabilize the client, process the trauma, and remain relationally connected.

Attending and Restorative Approaches

Counselors must further attend to signs of the client being triggered around the trauma narratives and to increases in negative behaviors. The counselor cannot always respond in a forthright manner to the trauma and complex trauma of traumatized people, particularly ALANAs, since direct confrontation of trauma experiences may result in decreased social interactions, increased difficulty with regulating emotions, increased detachment and impulse control, and negative impacts on self-esteem, shame, and guilty feelings.

Play therapy and art therapy are effective interventions to apply during attending sessions. Age-appropriate play and art therapy provide clients with developmentally appropriate activities to improve affect regulation, self-efficacy, problem solving, and relational trust. Trauma, play, and art therapy are useful because traumatized ALANA clients often lack the insight and verbal capacity to express and engage in talk therapy. Thus, drawing pictures or playing games—a board game, computer game, game of billiards, or game of HORSE on a basket-ball court—may provide an opportunity for nonverbal retelling and relaxing around the trauma experience. These comfortable, safe, and engaging strategies remove the pressure and change the counseling context to one that allows the therapeutic, emphatic, nurturing, and healing relationship to be central.

After enriching the therapeutic relationship, the counselor and client can then effectively journey together using interventions focused on repairing attachments, self-regulation, and building competence. A spoiler for those who have not seen *Moon Knight*—the hero suffers from a dissociative disorder (or, colloquially, he has multiple person-alities) because of his childhood trauma. In the episode discussed here the writers and director attempt to show the curative work of the counseling by depicting the healing between the dissociated personal-ities and the mother. This healing of the dissociation in turn leads to internal consoling and the development of a love between parts of the personality (Steven) and the wife.

Another attending and advantageous restorative treatment strategy with racially traumatized clients is rites-of-passage interven-tions, and these interventions are important and effective because they incorporate contexts into the intervention. A rites-of-passage program is a culturally based initiation program for young men and women to enter adulthood. These programs change the treatment lens of the intervention by addressing norms, prejudices, and intersectionality with their participants. They specifically address issues of racism and systemic oppression, are designed to be culturally responsive, and embrace the unique cultural context and conditions of clients. Since ALANAs do better in counseling when they are comfortable talking about their feelings and traumas, interventions that build on their cultural contexts are very effective.

Other rites-of-passage programs that have received widespread affirmation include martial-arts training and other sports-related activ-ities. These programs, typically with youth, seek to address concerns such as school suspension, social adjustment, and conflicts with educators, as well as goals like increasing academic performance, building self-confidence, and leadership development. Recently, more academically focused rites-of-passage interventions have included science, technology, engineering, and math (STEM) and science, technology, engineering, art, and math (STEAM) programs. Many programs include capstone projects and final community celebrations to allow participants to show mastery, build allies, and strengthen community.

Rites-of-passage programs also attend to intergenerational matters, attention that is critical to addressing racial trauma on a community level. Building on intergenerational relationships allows for the wisdom and experience of the elders to be shared with young participants in a palatable way, enabling the elder who has suffered trauma to appropriately share their skills and healing tips. Young people who have suffered oppression and trauma find alliance with freedom fighters and survivors from the previous generation, obtaining important stories and friendships. These programs provide trauma-informed counselors with the tools for addressing community violence and the lack of protective factors in the client's environment, and offer directions for adjusting our counseling and care to meets the needs of the client.

These programs are not in and of themselves the solution to the complex issues confronting race-, gender-, and class-oppressed clients. However, a trauma-informed therapist working with traumatized ALANA clients can draw on numerous strategies for self-knowledge and self-awareness, from art therapy and play therapy to restorative justice orientation and rites-of-passage program platforms and interventions. These strategies provide a way to reconceptualize our counseling in a fashion that connects with the client's culture and creates maps for advocacy and reconciliation. In my practice, the eclectic approach has been very helpful. Specifically, using racial socialization practices such as restorative justice and rites of passage have proved crucial.

To ask families about their cultural experiences or experiences with racial traumas is not a question of if but a question of when. When working with clients, I acknowledge that cultural differences and racial trauma exist even if the client does not share their race-related traumas with me. I thus seek to include affirmation and acknowledgment, make space for race, use race storytelling, validate and name racial experiences, minimize externalizing and devaluing, counteract devaluation, and always rechannel rage (both clients' and my own).[7] This eclectic race-informed approach to treating racially traumatized clients provides skill-training and problem-solving resources to the counselor and the client and it assists in the creation of the "holding space" and the development of the therapeutic relationship. These interventions foster healthy communities and successful counseling practices. This approach is counter to any approach that seeks to treat racially traumatic injuries with a general approach. Racially traumatic injuries are chronic conditions, and they indicate that the health condition of the client is long-lasting and persistent. They require a culturally appropriate approach to treating the wound to be effective.[8]

Every trauma injury is not the same. The trauma framework for intervention with ALANAs must expand assessment, conceptualization, application, and approach to be successful. Racially traumatized ALANA clients have experienced racial violence, bullying, and discrimination. They have often been made to feel unsafe in neighborhoods, and they may have been displaced from their home.[9] These realities complicate their lives and make the treatment more complex and demanding.

The mental health profession would be unnecessary if there were no mental, emotional, or traumatic events in human experience, and life would certainly be simpler if there was no racism and oppression, but humans live an existence that includes emotional and communal situations that positively and negatively affect how we act, think, and feel. As mental health professionals we must accept that mental health problems are common and linked to family, physiology, culture, and other important variables. Therefore, counselors must respond to the mental health of clients and help them forge meaning out of calamity.

The aged model of primary, secondary, and tertiary prevention and intervention is a useful conceptualization to organize our counseling efforts with all patients, including ALANAs. Primary prevention and intervention efforts are focused on preventing the mental health issue (or trauma) before it develops; secondary actions are attempts to detect the mental health issue (or trauma) early and intervene early; and tertiary endeavors are directed at managing the verified mental health issues (including traumas) in the ALANA client and avoiding further complications. Adding culturally appropriate variables and conceptualization to our prevention and intervention efforts with racially traumatized ALANA clients strengthens our effectiveness. Incorporating these sensibilities will improve the delivery of mental health care and strengthen the efficacy of cognitive and behavioral change strategies. Rather than having to justify the usefulness of their work with racialized trauma clients, counselors will be able to point confidently to the engaged, motivated, and recovering ALANA clients who have participated in and refer to their culturally appropriate trauma-informed interventions.

7

PATH TO SPIRITUAL WELLBEING

ONE DYNAMIC PATH to psycho-social-spiritual wellbeing comes through music. Eulaulah Donyll "Lalah" Hathaway is an American singer and the daughter of the late great American soul singer Donny Hathaway. Lalah was born December 16, 1968, and was ten years old when her father died tragically.

Lalah sings a song entitled "Mirror." The lyrics, written by James Morris, Guordan Banks, and David Gains, speak deeply, and when Lalah sings the song, there is a depth of spirit that touches the very soul of the listener. The words of one of the verses are:

> *Bitter hearts don't hold a smile*
> *Troubled minds will wear you down*
> *Use your past to get ahead*
> *Hold your tears and think instead*
> *You have to find a way to make it*
> *These clouds are letting up for a while.*
> *Sometimes you gotta make*
> *The mirror your best friend*
> *Maybe then, you'll find some peace within.*
> *Stop hiding yourself, stop hiding yourself*
> *Love yourself*
> *When no one else can.*

When Lalah sings, this listener hears an artist who understands pain and loss and has come to terms with both.[1] She brings an authenticity to the metaphor "make the mirror your best friend," because her rendition of "Mirror" reveals an insight into the deepest parts of the self (Chapter 5) and challenges the self to let go of its burdens.

At the time of writing, her YouTube video singing this song has been viewed 1,037,963 times, and the comments made by 546 viewers substantiate the power of the song.[2] Viewers consistently commented about how the lyrics spoke to their situations and that this song, as she sang it, helped to heal their souls. This type of soulful artistry holds a key to helping trauma-informed counselors work with ALANA clients.

I recall how music helped me work through the trauma of having lost a very close friend. Several years after the death of my friend, I awoke from sleep in the middle of the night feeling overwhelming sadness. I got up from the bed, walked into my study, picked up my trumpet from its stand, and placed the mute in the bell of the trumpet. I felt comfort as I held the horn close to my chest. I felt peace as I warmed up the mouthpiece and began fingering the keys. I felt more comfort as I began to play softly. I had played the trumpet sporadically for years after graduating from high school and was not as good as I used to be, but that night it was not about how well I could play, it was about healing. As I recalled memories of my dear friend, I played well and the melodies coming from my horn healed my soul. I do not remember if I played some of my old favorites, such as "Kinda Blue" by Miles Davis or Doc Severinsen's rendition of Count Basie's "Take the A Train." More important were the healing and the visitation. As I began to play, I accomplished my need to commune with my memories of my deceased friend. Playing the trumpet was my gateway to a memorial, and a mirror into my conscious and unconscious pain. I played and I cried, and I found closure for the loss I was grieving.

Like so many mental health professionals, I am accustomed to caring for others at the expense of myself. But on that night, some ten years after my friend died, I came face to face with the mirror and the music cared for me.

Psycho-Social-Spiritual Counseling Relationship

As with the sudden death of my friend, tragedy is an injury outside of our control and it activates our central nervous system's fight–flight–freeze protective reflex. A fighter responds with action; a person prone to flight tends to emotionally maneuver away from the traumatic situation; and a person who experiences a freeze response tends to habitually use a strategy interruption response to threats.

Trauma can result from unattended uncontrollable loss. In this condition trauma produces internal and external consequences. For ALANA clients, there is a cost to loss-based traumas resulting from centuries of neglect, manipulation, abuses, and racial violence toward Indigenous peoples, immigrants, and other people of color. The cost is high levels of poverty, high mortality rates, poor health care, and an ongoing list of other external injuries and internal consequences. Things have fallen apart in the treatment of racial trauma among ALANAs, and adopting a psychological-social-spiritual healing perspective is one strategy for improving our treatment of racial traumas. This counseling approach will serve to augment standard counseling practices and theories with culturally enhanced trauma-informed counseling practices and methods.

This enhanced trauma-informed counseling approach has been proven to be effective with ALANAs.[3] These practices and methods draw on the counselors' gifts and skills, social network, spiritual network, and knowledge of healing. For instance, in my late-night music session, the trumpet was the gift, playing was the skill, family was the social network, memories of my beloved friend were the spiritual network, and the music of my musical mentors was healing to the soul.

Like music, trauma-informed counseling can attend to the brokenness of ALANA clients who suffer with complex racial trauma. The integration of creative ideas and strategies presented in these pages represents years of laboring with the traumas of ALANA clients and serving as a supervisor and mentor to counselors working with this population. Mental health professionals who build on the wisdom and experience of standard counseling approaches and add trauma-informed counseling theory and guiding principles to their counseling practices will be more effective. Qualified mental health professionals who also undergird their treatment approach with trauma-informed materials are essential to our recovery from years of neglect and abuse of ALANAs. Additionally, mental health professionals will find more fulfillment and success in their counseling work with ALANAs if they incorporate the principles put forth in these pages into their practices.

There is a dearth of good counselors in our nation, with 65 percent of professional counselors reporting that they have no available appointment slots. Moreover, in excess of half of the people seeking mental health assistance report that they cannot find a therapist. The rate of seeking and not finding a counselor is even higher than 50 percent for ALANAs. People increasingly need mental health assistance and that need increases if you are ALANA seeking mental health counseling. This makes it imperative that when we do accept a client, particularly an ALANA client, we are equipped to successfully counsel them.

Universities with master's- and doctoral-level counseling and psychology programs should include, as a requirement for all students, a course on trauma-informed counseling. Seminaries could develop a license-eligible pastoral care and counseling program to better equip those called to pastoral care ministry and chaplaincy. The objectives for such a program might be the ability to equip participants to: (*i*) demonstrate the appropriate skills needed for counseling ministry in Christian and multifaith settings using the appropriate spiritual resources and practices of the Christian tradition and contextual theological reflection; (*ii*) demonstrate knowledge of and ability to appropriate major theories of counseling and psychotherapy and psychosocial and lifecycle development concepts in the ministerial practice of (pastoral) counseling; (*iii*) have knowledge of and the ability to utilize the *Diagnostic and Statistical Manual of Mental Disorders* (DSM-5) and developmental theory to diagnostically relate and therapeutically respond to a variety of (clients') counseling situations/issues; (*iv*) formulate a well-developed, collaborative counseling ministry project bearing evidence of being informed by methodologies of analytic, counseling theory, and ministerial research pertinent to their (counseling) context of ministry; and (*v*) demonstrate cultural competence, sensitivity to issues of difference (race, gender, age, economics, etc.,) and personal ethics, exhibiting growth in their counseling ministerial capacity and spiritual maturity.

Our reason for developing these types of programs would be their likelihood to address the shortage of mental health professionals serving ALANAs. The programs would also develop and equip ministers to work in community mental health centers. We would be positioned to provide hospital, prison, military, and community chaplains with additional mental health counseling skills. These fundamental counseling principles are critical to the development of these programs; however, understanding trauma, using art, and the heartful and mindful principles must also be added to the curriculum.

We have found that ALANA ministers are trusted by members of the ALANA community as second responders. The first call from the family in crisis is to 911. The second call made is to competent ministers. As second responders to trauma situations, ministers must learn to minimize client retraumatization, enhance trauma healing, and build resilience in traumatized ALANA clients. We must foster healing while avoiding harm and use our talents to abide with hurting people and find ways while learning to help them conquer the impact of their own trauma. We must care-front generational trauma and systemic oppression and racism.

When working with those who are frequently targeted and more apt to experience the trauma around fears of being betrayed, assaulted, or denied justice, we must adapt our methods and approaches through the knowledge of biological, psychological, social, and spiritual interventions. We must seek to understand the arousal patterns of unconscious trauma and the dynamics of conscious awareness, and develop compassionate relationships based on counseling strategies. Only from this standpoint can counselors confidently provide trauma-informed counseling with ALANA clients.

Bridge Builders

A crucial concern in conducting trauma-informed counseling must be the counselor–client relationship. Racial trauma is a relational wound and typically, in trauma cases, the client's trust in the system, community, and/or family has been destroyed. This breech in trust requires mending the torn threads of the relational tapestry. Trauma-informed counselors must provide a safe, trusting, and empowering space in which the injured client can explore renewal and healing.

As ALANA citizens face the struggles and challenges of living in a racially biased environment, we must bridge the relational gaps. ALANA clients must be empowered by the counseling relationship to prevent the ongoing persistent complex trauma from causing serious harm. To protect themselves and ensure safety and happiness, racially traumatized ALANA clients can develop defenses against racial, gender, and class attacks. The goal is to develop the clients' heartful and mindful awareness in a way that directs their internal emotions and promotes healing. This is accomplished by equipping ALANA clients with strategies enabling them to open their hearts and train their brains to caring instead of automatically responding in anger. Using mindfulness and heartfulness practices, the counselor can help the ALANA client practice loving kindness and harm reduction.[4]

Heartful and mindful healing processes help clients achieve harmony of mind, body, and spirit. These practices entail assisting clients who are triggered emotionally when they encounter "new" painful experiences to tap into an ability to be present with the hurtful thoughts, troubling emotions, and negative physical symptoms. As the counselor has the clients close their eyes and settle into a comfortable position and focus on being fully alive, the clients connect mind, body, and soul to positive existing. As clients recall feelings of positive living, they identify how it "feels" to be upbeat. Directing ALANA clients to draw a mental picture of positive living positions them to apply the experiences of positive living memories to the trauma of racial, gender, and class oppression. This approach is supportive of racially traumatized clients as they identify the persons involved in the development of their racial trauma. Discussing their feelings toward the perpetrators and then having them "gift" themselves and the perpetrator with the feelings of being alive and loved is healing.

This is not an easy exercise. I recall an incident from the time when I returned to Detroit after graduating from college to work and reconnect with my mother and siblings. I was jogging on Jefferson Avenue one morning singing and praying, when a pickup truck drove past me and a white male passenger yelled out the window, "N-Word get off the street and go back to your country!" The incident triggered my racial trauma and a gut-level defensive response. I felt threatened, and I did not respond with love or kindness. I did not turn the other cheek, and I did not pray for the man who had just verbally assaulted me. I was ready to fight using the heavy stick that I always carried with me when I ran outside. And the curse words I used were not words I would have wanted my mother to hear coming from my mouth. But, years later, I can reflect on that experience and have grown from the encounter. This healing occurred through personal and group counseling, as well as teaching and supervising other counselors engaged in this work. I can now use the memory of my trauma experiences in my work as a pastoral psychotherapist. I can think about my experiences in Detroit. I can focus on my interaction with a white colleague during my chaplaincy training who helped me and an African American family I was supporting during their crisis. I think of my relationship with white colleagues on faculty in a department of psychology that helped me heal from my distrust of white people. This grace is now a gift I can give to others.

It is times like these, when racial incidents trigger memories of racial assault, that substantiate the notion that ALANA trauma survivors must vigilantly focus on their recovery from racial traumas. I have grown to live with gratitude for those who trigger my racial trauma because those triggering experiences have helped me realize I am resilient and mentally healthy. But I may never be completely without the residual memories of racial incidents that can be triggered. Triggers can become alarm bells alerting the ALANA client of potential danger.

I also recall when my spouse and I were told by the FBI that our church was on the burn-down list of a white supremacist group. Rather than reacting with the fight, flight, or freeze response, we used our relationships and developed security measures. We contacted our friends on the police force and arranged programs and conversations with them about ways to protect ourselves and guarantee a response from them, the police. We had also begun to develop a relationship with the white Presbyterian pastor of a church a mile down the road. Serendipitously, the two congregations began building relationships of trust and goodwill through shared meals, meaningful conversations, joint sunrise Easter services, and field trips. When police shootings heightened racial tensions in our country, the pastors of both churches began to question, "How can we give our people space to process these issues together?" We developed a joint program we named Bridge Builders. The Bridge Builders' mission statement was, "Together promoting relationships to help build a racially, divinely just and inclusive society." A steering committee was formed that consisted of eight persons, four from each church, along with the pastors. Bridge Builders grew to become a group of fifty persons, twenty-five from each church, who would come together, first to get acquainted as neighbors. The group met monthly throughout the year, alternating church sites, to build relationships of trust and to have discussions about the racial climate in our community. Over the years, we saw relationships form, and we noticed that, with every luncheon, our conversations grew deeper and more honest. After some months of conversation and relationship building, we took a field trip together and walked Richmond's Slave Trail. This field trip was a significant catalyst for racial reconciliation and discussion. During this program we learned to reflect on the fact that our Black and white neighbors were subject to the same emotional experiences of joy, love, sorrow, and grief.

As the members of both congregations learned to appreciate one another and focused intently on maintaining an open heart of care for others with different skin tones and cultures, we saw barriers lifting. Moreover, as Bridge Builders participants learned to empathize with the painful experiences of their neighbors, forgiveness and reconciliation was possible. The pastors even noticed that body language during difficult conversations shifted from defensive and irritated postures to encouraging and engaging postures.

I remember a cathartic shifting that took place during one of the luncheons when one of the African American matriarchs stood and told stories of how she worked as a nurse during the March to Selma and witnessed "Bloody Sunday." She spoke of how, after marching all day, she and other marchers slept in tents at night and how she feared for her own life and the lives of others, though they were determined to keep marching for their freedom and equality as American citizens. As she told her story, you could hear sniffles and see people wiping their eyes and shaking their heads in disbelief. We all learned of her fear and bravery and felt compassion for her and the other freedom fighters. It was especially rewarding to observe the impact her stories had on the young people of both congregations.

Bridge Builders was a program that taught us to share one another's sorrows. We helped one another respond with compassion and not guilt. We developed into wounded healers and warrior healers. Some white members of the program later dedicated their lives to working toward racial justice, equity, and inclusion. Black Americans of the Bridge Builders group learned to cope and survive with racial trauma as descendants of enslaved people. This is the definition of post-traumatic growth (PTG): "positive psychological changes experienced as a result of the struggles with traumatic or highly challenging life circumstances."[5]

It is easy to see people who are struggling as fundamentally broken. Trauma, which increases anxiety and depression, leads to irritability and withdrawal, making it hard for the affected person to find joy. At these times, an ALANA client may long to dispel their brokenness and become a "whole" person, but that type of wholeness contains only the conscious, unpainful, welcomed parts of the self. The goal of effective trauma-informed therapy is to help the client realize that their brokenness is not the opposite of their wholeness; the two are important components of the healthy self. Counseling focused on racially traumatized ALANA clients must repair the broken part(s) of the self and reintegrate them into the acceptable, welcomed parts of the self. This broken part of the self is the shadow self.[6] This self contains the hidden, rejected, and repressed human thoughts and emotions. It is the dissociated and traumatized self, the thing(s) a person has no wish to be.[7] One cannot be a whole self without embracing the shadow self along with the welcomed self.

The *kintsugi* art shown on this book's cover is a metaphor for a repaired shadow self, integrated and welcomed as a whole self. In *kintsugi*, the porcelain fractures of a work of art are repaired with varnish or with gold and, as with humans, breaks and repairs are part of the object's history. What *kintsugi* does, and what is recommended for trauma-informed counseling with ALANA clients, is to show and not hide the scars. *Kintsugi* embellishes the breaks in the art pieces and treats them as an important part of the object's history. The formerly broken object, then, is not something disposable but is a precious object to be valued more than ever. This embellishing of the treasure, of healed ALANAs, is the aim of trauma-informed counseling. The aim is to knit the welcomed self with the broken self to become a priceless self. We must teach racially traumatized ALANA clients to show the transformation of their trauma scars to themselves and to their perpetrators.

Another *kintsugi*-like story that has many variations is the one about a parent and a child: The parent receives a beautiful book as a gift. The parent is upset when the child gets a crayon and draws on one of the book's pages. Out of anger the parent scolds the child. Years later, when the parent comes across the book and sees the child's drawing, the parent realizes that the "graffitied" page is the most precious page in the book. What initially seemed to be damaged goods had become the treasure.

The lines our clients draw between broken and whole are false distinctions. Each client we counsel is a complete individual with shadow thoughts, feelings, and broken dreams, particularly those clients who suffer from racially traumatic experiences. Yet they are also individuals who have unique passions, ideas, and hope-filled dreams. Our task is to be *kintsugi* artists, helping our clients realize that the self is made better by both the welcomed and the broken experiences. As an alternative to thinking of the self as broken, we can help clients remember their racial traumas and then integrate their brokenness with their celebrated self. Chloé Cooper Jones makes this argument to remember and then integrate in her description of easy and difficult beauty.[8] "Easy beauty" are those activities we consciously call beautiful, and "difficult beauty" are those mundane, messy, and "ugly" places and spaces we seek to avoid.

The radical reframing of presence is the powerful intervention that combines difficult and easy beauty. My mother has always characterized her single mother role with my six siblings and me as "blessed." Since my earliest memories she has referred to her seven children as the magnificent seven. I am proud to be affectionally known as Mag 1.

Several years ago, Samuel (Mag 2) was released after forty years of incarceration. He returned home to live with our mother in Detroit. Upon his release our brother Robert (Mag 4) took two months off from work to stay with Samuel and Mom, assisting with Samuel's reentry. It was an exciting time. We celebrated family and survival. Our son, brother, cousin, and friend had made it home. After that July release, Samuel worked two jobs and did well integrating himself into his new life.

Then tragedy struck. On Christmas Day, just five months after Samuel's release, Richard (Mag 5 and Robert's twin) was hospitalized. The physicians reported to the family that Richard was suffering from stage four pancreatic cancer. They were not optimistic about his chances to live long; in fact, they instructed his wife to call the family to the hospital. After everyone said their teary goodbyes, the physicians placed Richard in a medically induced coma. Richard died six days later, on New Year's Eve.

We were devastated. We had no idea that our brother was ill— no clue that Richard was suffering from the deadly disease of pancreatic cancer. To complicate the loss, New Year's Eve is the birthday of Samuel (Mag 2), his first since returning home from incarceration. A birthday celebration for Samuel had already been planned, a party Samuel wanted to cancel in the wake of Richard's death. But our mother vetoed the idea of cancellation and told the family we needed to celebrate. As our family gathered that evening, we grieved the loss of Richard and celebrated the freedom of Samuel. We mourned Richard's physical absence and showered Samuel with love and acceptance. During the dinner, our mother rose from her seat, clanged a spoon against her water glass, cleared her throat, and announced to the family that she had something to say. I will always remember her words that evening. My mother turned to Samuel, looked directly at him, and began speaking these words to him:

> *Samuel, Richard's dying on your birthday was not an*
> *accident, it was a God-wink. It was Richard saying to you,*
> *I must go, man, but I am passing the responsibility of taking*
> *care of Mom to you. Samuel, you are the only McCreary man*
> *left here in Detroit with me. Both Micah and Robert live in*
> *other states. So, Richard is telling you from heaven, no more*
> *foolishness and no more bad decisions—your mother is now*
> *your responsibility!*

I still remember looking at Samuel's face as Mom made that statement. Her speech was a powerful reframe. Her words connected the ugly with the beautiful; they remembered the broken story with the welcomed memories. I could see the tears and the realization in Samuel's eyes as he balanced his losses and his responsibilities.

Yes, Samuel had lived through racial trauma and the difficulties of incarceration. But the radical reframe of my mother left an indelible positive mark on his life and behavior. Living with his "demons" and not fighting against them, he is a better and more complete brother. Two powerful outcomes of this story are the creation of a family chat that keeps all of us connected and the holding of our first family reunion in over forty years. As Samuel and I stood by the river listening to Sam Cooke's "A Change Is Gonna Come," I was thinking, thank God the change has come.

Samuel and I have always resonated with "Invictus,"[9] a poem written by W. E. Henley in 1875:

> *Out of the night that covers me,*
> *Black as the pit from pole to pole,*
> *I thank whatever gods may be*
> *For my unconquerable soul.*
>
> *In the fell clutch of circumstance*
> *I have not winced nor cried aloud.*
> *Under the bludgeonings of chance*
> *My head is bloody, but unbowed.*
>
> *Beyond this place of wrath and tears*
> *Looms but the Horror of the shade,*
> *And yet the menace of the years*
> *Finds and shall find me unafraid.*
>
> *It matters not how strait the gate,*
> *How charged with punishments the scroll,*
> *I am the master of my fate,*
> *I am the captain of my soul.*

The word *invictus* is Latin for "unconquerable," and Henley wrote this poem about stoicism, courage, and the refusal to accept defeat while enduring a testing hospitalization. He had contracted tuberculosis of the bone in his youth, and his lower leg was amputated in his twenties.

Samuel has resonated with the unconquerable aspect of the poem, but we struggled with the lines thanking whatever gods may be, being the master of our fates, and being the captains of our souls. Our tragedies and triumphs have taught us that it takes effort and grace to overcome. For us and many others, living with racial trauma means fighting the night that covers us until we are captains. To be unconquerable entails addressing fundamental needs and performing concrete human acts.

As victors over racial trauma, "unconquerable" means choosing life over death. We must not allow our clients to put their painful life experiences in boxes. Traumatic experiences will remain life's triggers until "trauma-victors" master sitting with pain and integrating it with joy. This integration of our trauma experiences—of brokenness and welcoming, of difficult and easy beauty, and of rejecting and reframing—is successful failing forward and is a critical skill when emerging from trauma.

Psychodrama and Paradox

We have addressed psychological and social wellbeing, referring to one's overall emotional functioning and group functioning respectively. Spiritual wellbeing focuses on one's sense of purpose and meaning. It is a concern about integrity, ethics, and morality.[10] Addressing an ALANA client's psychological, social, and spiritual wellbeing provides the counselor with complex tools to confront a complex challenge. Let me share an illustration on one method to engage the psycho-social-spiritual complexities in trauma-informed counseling.

A woman once brought her two grandsons to counseling. She sought help for their behavior, which she described as being out of control. The schoolteachers and administrators at the school the eleven-year-old and nine-year-old boys attended were also overwhelmed by the brothers' challenging behaviors. To develop therapeutic bonds with the boys and understand their situation, the counselors visited the boys at school and at church and spent time playing pool and taking walks to the campus bookstore with them.

In our counseling sessions, the grandmother mentioned that she had been raising the boys alone since their mother died from a drug overdose. She informed us that she had been their guardian for four years and felt that she was too lenient. The boys had little to say, sitting there with guilty looks on their faces that soon turned to mischievous glances and smiles. From this behavior, it was clear the grandsons knew what they were doing, and they had control over their emotions and thinking.

My co-counselor and I then began addressing the trauma they experienced around the loss of their mother (and father). The younger brother began to cry during these discussions and, at some point, his older brother would crack jokes or say something disparaging about "drugheads." The two would then fall over laughing while the grandmother looked to the counselors for assistance.

I then asked the boys, "Do the drugheads in your neighborhood remind you of your mother?" They replied that they didn't know. The grandmother responded by discussing how wonderful her daughter was before she became addicted to crack cocaine. She told the boys that their mother was a brilliant student and a gifted athlete. She shared that the oldest grandson had his mother's athletic ability, and the youngest grandson had her intelligence and sensitivity. Then in passing she said, "But the way you two boys act is killing me."

I asked the boys, "Why are you trying to kill your grandmother?" They emphatically said they were not trying to kill her, that they loved her. I suggested they prove they loved their grandmother and did not want to kill her by behaving at school in a way that made her proud of them. I asked grandmother, "Are you okay if they behave in school and misbehave a little at home?" She said if they behaved in school and church, they could act any way they wanted at home. The boys readily accepted the challenge.

Not surprisingly, in the next session, we learned that the misbehavior increased for the oldest grandson at school and for the younger grandson at church. It was reported that the boys acted like angels at home. When we asked the boys for an explanation, they pretended that they had done their best and would do better the next week.

My co-counselor and I processed our observations with the family. We asked the boys how was it that they had been so excited about the challenge for the week, yet did absolutely none of what they said they would do? As expected, they both answered with silly looks and shoulder shrugs. So, we discussed that one grandson behaved at school and one behaved at church, but both behaved at home. The next week, the boys reported that they both failed to behave in school and at home; their grandmother was too tired to take them to church.

Well, this outcome was unacceptable. The boys had failed their grandmother and themselves. They had, in fact, killed their grandmother; the funeral was all that was left. So, I asked grandmother to "die on the sofa." After the grandmother metaphorically died on the sofa in the counseling room, the boys had to walk to the coffin and say their goodbyes to her. They were told they could leave the "funeral room" and step outside to the counseling lobby for one minute if they needed to (where a graduate student was present to supervise). The condition for leaving, however, was that they had to tell us what they were feeling and thinking before and after they left the room. Apparently, leaving the room and their grandmother was emotionally unacceptable, so they remained present in the psychodrama.

Their grandmother also played along with the psychodrama, but we could see tears running from her closed eyes. The play acting was a lot for the emotionally concrete, immature boys to deal with, but they were determined to win the game and stay cool. However, the technique triggered their attachment trauma around the loss of their parents, particularly their mother. The reframe of their misbehavior as causing the death of their grandmother, the only family to take them in and care for them, finally slipped past their defenses. The younger grandson began to cry, and the older grandson became very angry.

At this point my co-counselor and I asked them what they could do to bring their grandmother back to them. Both grandsons emphatically proclaimed that they could "act right." We spent the next phase of counseling helping them develop the skills needed to keep their promises to their grandmother and to themselves. We also worked to resolve their attachment traumas and channel their energy into their talents.

The psychodrama communicated meaning that words alone were unable to transmit. Drama is spiritual and it is spectacle. The psychodrama revealed the intensity of their emotions but was perceived by the boys as "play-acting" and not "real." The experience was intense but not as intense as institutionalization, which was being recommended by the school and other agencies. We did not expect the psychodrama to uncover the multigenerational transmission of trauma,[11] but in retrospect something of the magnitude of generational trauma had to exist for the system to remain so challenging.

The trauma of the grandsons was transmitted across generations. Their trauma was originated and built over several generations and was carried forward by their fore-parents. The past traumas were present in the room with this family, a dynamic that holds true for many ALANA families laboring with racial trauma. The pain of this grandmother was passed down to her by her mother and her mother's mother, and she in turn passed the trauma pain down to her daughter, who passed it down to her sons. This multigenerational family trauma was in both nature and intensity very painful, and the family's trauma found a conduit, conscious and unconscious, in the memories and painful interactions of this family. This family's system was governed by trauma, which we used to care-front the paralyzing behavior of the grandmother (born from trauma) and now was manifested as acting out traumatic behaviors by the grandsons. Emotionally and behaviorally, this family was cut off—cut off from sharing their grief, cut off from expressing their love, and cut off from their extended family. But the grandmother's love for her daughter and her grandsons cried out loudly, "I believe we can be better." As their counselors, we realized clinically and intuitively that this grandmother's quest for wholeness was a request for liberation.

We concluded that even more than helping the grandsons understand how much their grandmother missed their mother, it was critical for the sons to reconnect with the loss of their mother and face the trauma they carried. The possibility of losing their grandmother was the trigger we used to ignite a desire to live for the family and to love the family. Thus, the goal of the psychodrama was to eliminate the permanent separation from mother and grandmother and care-front the multigenerational transmission of racial traumas.

Of course, this psychodrama was effective only because the counselors had dealt with their own multigenerational trauma issues. We were willing, no matter how painful it was, to visit our own families-of-origin traumas, and we continually work on our own unfinished generational family trauma. In trauma-free families, much of the stress is not carried from one generation to the next. This is not the case with multigenerational traumatized families, whose traumas are always present and always debilitating. Using a multigenerational trauma transmission frame, counselors can work with racially traumatized ALANA clients to better predict trauma symptoms, recognize recycled patterns of avoidance and generalization, and identify where the trauma began. Moreover, the counselor working from a multigenerational trauma transmission frame can better gauge the various aspects of the trauma simultaneously. The trauma-informed counselor is then able to monitor the emotional, behavioral, social, and spiritual dimensions of the trauma. To adopt a multigenerational trauma transmission counseling frame is not a miracle cure. It is a lens into the pain caused by hierarchies, domination, and societal resistance to change. It is a search for the malignant cancer that needs to be cut out and have its fast-growing cells destroyed.

The multigenerational transmitted traumas experienced by the woman and her grandsons required a creative, systemic approach. If we were going to assist this family in their trauma recovery, we had to assume that the generational trauma had spread through the entire family system from one generation to the next. We thus approached treatment from a perspective that these clients had developed multiple family participants who were performing parts of the "trauma dance" repeatedly. As counseling continued, the grandmother was willing to pay the exorbitant cost of full transparency and vulnerability with her grandsons and with herself. She was able to tell her grandsons the big secret: she had "put their mother out" because of her addictive behaviors, and she felt responsible for their mother's death. She also told them of their father's physical abuse of their mother and how he was killed in a failed robbery attempt. This grandmother's honesty broke the generational transmission of secrets and lies, creating healing space for her and her grandsons.

We have found that systemic multigenerational counseling with racially traumatized ALANA clients justifies the psychological-social-spiritual expenses that clients must pay. Bottom-line, we are engaged in a battle for the souls of our clients. By the soul, I am referring to the true essence of the family and the client. This counseling work engages the true self (Chapter 1) of the counselor and the client, that aspect of the self that contains the positive, creative energy of life. This authentic counseling relationship searches for a "Self" greater than our little selves and bigger than our trauma problems. Here, truth, integrity, and grace abound. It's this core self of the counselor and the client that must be empowered to transform ALANA families beyond race, gender, and class traumas.

CONCLUSION

Counseling ALANAs at the intersection of race and trauma is a critical undertaking. ALANAs facing the difficulties of living with systemic racism in America have the added challenge of contending with the difficulties inherent in trauma. The mental, emotional, and spiritual wellbeing of ALANA clients is exacerbated by the interaction of race and trauma. Mental health professionals engaged in counseling racially traumatized ALANA clients must be trauma-informed and skilled in conducting counseling at the intersection of race and trauma.

The strategies and approaches suggested throughout this book are aimed primarily toward trauma-informed counseling at the intersection of race and trauma. Specifically, a trauma-informed therapeutic blueprint is offered and illustrated using clinical examples. This blueprint has five major counseling propositions.

First, counselors working with race and trauma must use a trauma-informed plan or blueprint to address the trauma issues and how they intersect with racial issues. There is undeniable evidence that systemic racism has impacted the core of existence in the United States.[1] For more than four hundred years, this country has created and tolerated a system that stole occupied lands from Indigenous peoples, enslaved people of African descent, excluded people of Spanish descent, and legally alienated people of Asian descent.[2] Thus, in addition to the struggle against manifest destiny, white supremacy, eugenics, Black codes, Black laws, and white nationalism, ALANA clients must also contend with trauma as it relates to systemic racism. It is the knowledge of the interaction between the trauma experienced and the confounding issues of racism that is critical to the practice of trauma-informed counseling with racially traumatized ALANA clients.

Second, racial trauma is complex trauma. Another way to examine the phenomenon of race and trauma is to conceptualize it as complex trauma. That is, the interactions of race and trauma begin with the realization that socio-race and trauma are both stressors and the combination of race and trauma makes this a complex stressor. Trauma is a product of exposure to actual or threatening danger, serious injury, or sexual violence. It is not necessarily a disorder, but it is always a stressor. Together the stressors of race and trauma result in complex trauma that can manifest itself with symptoms of reexperiencing, avoiding, and sensing traumatic threat. ALANAs with race and trauma experiences often remain wounded by past and present psycho-social-spiritual injuries. These injuries are complex. They are complex traumas.

Third, it is essential to establish a culturally appropriate counseling relationship. Establishing positive high-quality therapeutic relationships with ALANA clients will help the counselor counteract the cultural distrust that many of these clients have toward counseling. A quality therapeutic relationship positions the trauma-informed counselor to treat the mental health, race, and trauma issues (complex trauma), and this complex counseling situation necessitates the maintenance of the therapeutic relationship. It requires the trauma-informed counselor to be adept in self-awareness, self-examination, self-forgiveness, establishing transparency, and risk taking. This will allow the counselor to create safe counseling relationships and embrace the painful experiences of race and trauma.

Fourth, trauma-informed counselors must broaden their clinical and counseling frameworks. They must remain current and use appropriate best practices and empirically validated treatment strategies. They must expand their theoretical framework with important and creative ideas and notions in order to be effective in their treatment of complex trauma (socio-race and trauma). This counseling must accommodate the sociological issues surrounding the treatment of trauma and socio-race. The expanded therapeutic approach will add depth to the trauma-informed counselor's understanding of the interaction of race and trauma.

Fifth and finally, trauma-informed counseling must include a focus on spiritual wellbeing, and trauma-informed counselors must address issues such as forgiveness and reconciliation to counsel the whole person. Trauma counseling, race-based counseling, and complex race and trauma counseling each entail assisting ALANA clients in their struggles to forgive themselves and their perpetrators, as well as to reconcile with their racially traumatic experiences. Thus trauma-informed counseling must help clients to realize that human suffering is an insidious painful instrument of life that must be addressed, endured, and conquered. The psycho-social-spiritual path with ALANA clients is a mixture of goodness and heartbreak, of hatred and love. Trauma-informed counselors cannot regulate the experiences of their ALANA clients, but can assist them to learn and grow from their tragedy and turn tragedies into triumphs. Such counselors and racially traumatized ALANA clients strive to build a radical agape love that detoxifies the soul. This detox process avails the consciousness of counselor and client to understand more deeply the complexities of race and trauma, and ALANA clients are helped to explore human frailty and resilience.

Counseling at the intersection of race and trauma is counseling in the face of the interlocking systems of oppression that plague our social systems and the stress-based mental health challenges of trauma. This counseling entails confronting the defeatist mentality that results when an ALANA client is unable to control their trauma experience. By care-fronting fear-based and self-sabotaging behaviors, trauma-informed counselors can help ALANA clients replace trauma memories with life-sustaining, problem-solving, and healing thoughts. For a trauma-informed counselor to assist an ALANA client to examine the manufactured concept of race that systemically oppressed them and the mortifying situations of trauma that were the result offers a counseling approach that is effective and powerful enough to extinguish the trauma pain and usher in the healing presence of recovery. As we tend the wounds of racial trauma, may we step forward in freedom as revolutionary healers.

ABOUT THE AUTHOR

Rev. Micah L. McCreary, PhD, is the twelfth president of New Brunswick Theological Seminary and has served in this role since July 2017. Dr. McCreary, a native of Detroit, Michigan, came to NBTS from Richmond, Virginia, where he was President and CEO of McCreary and Madison Associates, Incorporated, a psychological and human resources consulting firm. Dr. McCreary also worked as a tenured Associate Professor of Psychology at Virginia Commonwealth University (VCU) for twenty-one years. During his career at VCU, Dr. McCreary held other positions, including his service as Assistant Vice Provost for Diversity, Quality Enhancement Plan Coordinator, and Co-Director of the Counseling Psychology Program.

Dr. McCreary is a member of the New Brunswick Classis of the Reformed Church in America. He was ordained by the New Hope Baptist Church in Ann Arbor, Michigan, a member of the National Baptist Convention, and his ordination was recognized by the American Baptist Churches in 2001 and received by the RCA in 2018. Dr. McCreary and his wife, the Reverend Dr. Jacqueline E. Madison-McCreary, pastored the Spring Creek Baptist Church in Moseley, Virginia for sixteen years. Prior to Spring Creek, Dr. McCreary was Director of Youth Ministry for the Baptist General Convention of Virginia and Senior Pastor of the Rising Mount Zion Baptist Church of Sandston, Virginia. The McCrearys are the parents of one adult daughter, Makeda McCreary.

Dr. McCreary holds a Bachelor of Science in engineering from the University of Michigan, a Master of Divinity degree from the Samuel DeWitt Proctor School of Theology, Virginia Union University, and a Master of Science and PhD in counseling psychology from Virginia Commonwealth University. Dr. McCreary has received several fellowships, including the American Psychological Association Minority Fellowship, the State Council of Higher Education in Virginia Fellowship, and the American Council on Education Presidential Fellowship. His work includes grants and contracts to promote better health among families affected by substance abuse, and he has published numerous articles and book chapters on his teaching, service, and research.

NOTES

Introduction

1 https://www.pewabic.org/pages/about.
2 Jeremiah 18:1–10 (NRSV).

Chapter 1

1 P. L. Mason, *Encyclopedia of Race and Racism*, 2nd ed. (Farmington, MI: Gale, 2013), 1:xi–xiii.
2 A recent example of Americans discouraging critical dialogue is reflected in the opposition to teaching diversity and inclusion in local schools: https://www.journalinquirer.com/connecticut_and_region/opponents-of-critical-race-theory-seek-to-flip-school-boards/article_da4c804e-3587-11ec-82e6-eb2c8d94fc3f.html.
3 The 1867 Reconstruction Act divided the South into five military districts and outlined how new governments, based on manhood suffrage without regard to socio-race, were to be established. Thus began the period of Radical or Congressional Reconstruction, which lasted until the end of the last Southern Republican governments in 1877 (https://www.britannica.com/event/Reconstruction-United-States-history#ref226042).
4 R. Chernow, *Grant* (New York: Penguin, 2017), 377, 588–701.
5 L. F. Litwack, "HellHounds," in *Without Sanctuary: Lynching Photography in America*, ed. J. Allen (Santa Fe, NM: Twin Palms, 2020), 8–37.
6 Litwack, *Without Sanctuary*, 10–12.
7 Litwack, 10–12.
8 Black codes were laws passed in the South that gave police the authority to govern formerly enslaved people. Black codes foreshadowed Jim Crow laws and included the establishment of

systems that governed movement, ensured cheap labor for factories, established vagrancy laws, and made it a criminal offense not to work. See D. A. Blackmon, *Slavery by Another Name* (New York: Knopf Doubleday, 2008), loc. 124, Kindle; and N. Hannah-Jones, *The 1619 Project: A New American Origin Story* (New York: Random House, 2021) (Kindle).

9 See Blackmon, *Slavery by Another Name.*

10 I. Wilkerson, *The Warmth of Other Suns: The Epic Story of America's Great Migration* (New York: Knopf Doubleday, 2010) (Kindle).

11 Wilkerson, *The Warmth of Other Suns,* 10.

12 Mason, *Encyclopedia of Race and Racism,* 1:xx–xxi.

13 Mason, 1:xi–xiii.

14 The term "revolt" or "revolution" is purposefully used here. The common term used for these events is "riots." However, a riot is a violent offense against public order and involves the gathering of people for illegal purposes. A revolt is an overt act of defiance. And a revolution constitutes a challenge to the established political order and the eventual establishment of a new order radically different from the preceding one.

15 L. A. Slavin, K. L. Rainer, M. L. McCreary, and K. K. Gowda, "Toward a Multicultural Model of the Stress Process," *Journal of Counseling and Development* 70, no. 1 (September 1991): 156.

16 R. S. Lazarus, *Psychological Stress and Coping Process* (New York: Springer, 1966); R. S. Lazarus and S. Folkman, *Stress, Appraisal, and Coping* (New York: Springer, 1984).

17 https://hbr.org/2016/04/are-you-too-stressed-to-be-productive-or-not-stressed-enough.

18 American Psychiatric Association, *Diagnostic and Statistical Manual of Mental Disorders,* 3rd ed. (Washington, DC: American Psychiatric Association, 1980), 236.

19 Hannah-Jones, *The 1619 Project,* 392, 406, 466–67, 549.

Chapter 2

1 M. L. King Jr., "Behavioral Scientist in the Civil Rights Movement," invited distinguished address presented to the meeting of the Society for Psychological Study of Social Issues, American Psychological Association, Washington, DC, 1967.

2 K. W. Crenshaw, "Demarginalizing the Intersection of Race and Sex: A Black Feminist Critique of Antidiscrimination Doctrine, Feminist Theory and Antiracism Politics," *University of Chicago Legal Forum* 1989, no. 1: 140, 139–67.

3 https://www.lexico.com/en/definition/intersectionality.

4 I. Wilkerson, *Caste: The Origins of Our Discontents* (New York: Random House, 2020), loc. 17, Kindle.

5 Mason, *Encyclopedia of Race and Racism*, 3:413–65; B. D. Tatum, *"Why Are All the Black Kids Sitting Together in the Cafeteria?" and Other Conversations About Race* (New York: Basic Books, 1997), 408–24.

6 P. H. Collins, *Black Feminist Thought: Knowledge, Consciousness, and the Politics of Empowerment*, 2nd ed. (New York: Routledge, 2000).

7 Mason, 3:413–65.

8 L. Smith and S. Mao, "Social Class and Psychology," in *APA Handbook of Counseling Psychology*, vol. I: *Theories, Research, and Methods*, ed. N. A. Fouad, J. A. Carter, and L. M. Subich (Washington, DC: American Psychological Association, 2012), 523–40.

9 A. Freud, *The Ego and the Mechanisms of Defense* (London: Hogarth Press and Institute of Psycho-Analysis, 1937).

10 L. Comas-Díaz, G. N. Hall, and H. A. Neville, "Racial Trauma Theory, Research, and Healing: Introduction to Special Issue," *American Psychologist* 74, no. 1 (2019): 1–5.

11 S. Beaumont, *How to Lead When You Don't Know Where You're Going: Leading in a Liminal Season* (Lanham, MD: Rowman & Littlefield, 2019).

Chapter 3

1 Dr. Jack Corazzini, personal communication.

2 I. D. Yalom, *The Theory and Practice of Group Psychotherapy*, 3rd ed. (New York: Basic Books, 1986); P. Freire, *Pedagogy of the Oppressed* (New York: Bloomsbury, 1970).

3 B. L. Duncan, S. D. Miller, B. E. Wampold, and M. A. Hubble, eds., *The Heart and Soul of Change: Delivering What Works in*

Therapy, 2nd ed. (Washington, DC: American Psychological Association, 2011) (Kindle).

4 Duncan et al., *The Heart and Soul of Change,* 63.

5 To protect the client and the counselor, especially in this age of sexual harassment awareness, I also requested and received permission from guardians before escorting an adolescent to places outside of the counseling room. My offices also had windows in or around the door to allow visibility inside the counseling room.

6 Duncan et al., 63.

7 https://www.sciencedirect.com/science/article/abs/pii/0732 118X9190042K.

8 American Psychological Association, Presidential Task Force on Evidence-Based Practice, "Evidence-Based Practice in Psychology," *American Psychologist* 61, no. 4 (2006): 271–85.

9 American Psychiatric Association, *Diagnostic and Statistical Manual of Mental Disorders,* 5th ed. (Washington, DC: American Psychiatric Association, 2013), 274, https://ebooks.appi.org/epubreader/ diagnostic-statistical-manual-mental-disorders-dsm5.

10 *Diagnostic and Statistical Manual of Mental Disorders,* 5th ed., 21.

11 *Diagnostic and Statistical Manual of Mental Disorders,* 5th ed., 21.

12 M. Cloitre, "ICD-11 Complex Posttraumatic Stress Disorder: Simplifying Diagnosis in Trauma Populations," *The British Journal of Psychiatry* 216 (2020): 129–31. DOI: 10.1192/ bjp.2020.43.

13 Cloitre, "ICD-11 Complex Posttraumatic Stress Disorder."

14 J. Briere, *Psychological Assessment of Adult Posttraumatic States: Phenomenology, Diagnosis, and Measurement,* 2nd ed. (Washington, DC: American Psychological Association, 2004) (Kindle); B. A. van der Kolk, "Developmental Trauma Disorder: Toward a Rational Diagnosis for Children with Complex Trauma Histories," *Psychiatric Annals* 35, no. 5 (2005): 401–8.

15 J. E. Helms, G. Nicolas, and C. E. Green, "Racism and Ethnoviolence as Trauma: Enhancing Professional Training," *Traumatology* 16 (2010): 53–62.

16 Wilkerson, *Caste,* 17.

17 T. Bryant-Davis and C. Ocampo, "Racist Incident-Based Trauma," *The Counseling Psychologist* 33 (2005): 479–500.

18 A. Jennings, *Models for Developing Trauma-Informed Behavioral Health Systems and Trauma-Specific Services* (Washington, DC: National Technical Assistance Center, National Association of State Mental Health Program Directors, Center for Mental Health Services, Substance Abuse and Mental Health Services Administration, US Department of Health and Human Services, 2004).

19 D. E. Elliot, P. Bjelajac, R. D. Fallot, L. S. Markoff, and B. G. Reed, "Trauma-Informed or Trauma-Denied: Principles and Implementation of Trauma-Informed Services for Women," *Journal of Community Psychology* 33, no. 4 (2005): 461–77.

20 https://div12.org/importance-of-addressing-internalized-racism-in-clinical-practice-scp-diversity-committee/.

21 T. Clinton and G. Sibcy, *Attachments* (Brentwood, TN: Thomas Nelson, 2002), 24.

Chapter 4

1 https://www.edweek.org/leadership/what-is-critical-race-theory-and-why-is-it-under-attack/2021/05; https://www.nytimes.com/interactive/2019/08/14/magazine/1619-america-slavery.html.

2 W. Self, "A Posthumous Shock," *Harper's Magazine*, December 2021, https://harpers.org/archive/2021/12/a-posthumous-shock-trauma-studies-modernity-how-everything-became-trauma/.

3 S. Joseph, *What Doesn't Kill Us* (New York: Basic Books, 2013), loc. 54, Kindle.

4 https://www.goodreads.com/author/quotes/7919.Richard_Rohr?page=2.

5 H. J. M. Nouwen, *The Wounded Healer: Ministry in Contemporary Society* (New York: Doubleday Dell, 1979) (Kindle).

6 For more on the modern science of the unconscious read L. Mlodinow, *Subliminal: How Your Unconscious Mind Rules You* (New York: Knopf Doubleday, 2012) (Kindle).

7 Mlodinow, *Subliminal.*

8 Supervision and training received while interning at Philadelphia Child Guidance Center, Children's Hospital, Philadelphia Pennsylvania, 1992.

9 https://www.berea.edu/cgwc/the-power-of-sankofa/.

10 Beaumont, *How to Lead When You Don't Know Where You're Going*, 114–21.
11 Beaumont, 29.
12 P. Freire, *Pedagogy of the Oppressed: 30th Anniversary Edition* (New York: Bloomsbury, 2000) (Kindle). Orig. pub. 1970, 1993.
13 bell hooks, *Teaching to Transgress: Education as the Practice of Freedom* (New York: Taylor and Francis, 1994) (Kindle).
14 J. L. Winek, *Systemic Family Therapy: From Theory to Practice* (Thousand Oaks, CA: Sage, 2010), 47.
15 Winek, *Systemic Family Therapy*, 43.
16 https://www.prayerfoundation.org/dailyoffice/serenity_prayer_full_version.htm.
17 https://www.hazeldenbettyford.org/articles/the-serenity-prayer.
18 https://www.hazeldenbettyford.org/articles/the-serenity-prayer.
19 H. J. M. Nouwen, *In the Name of Jesus: Reflection on Christian Leadership* (New York: Crossroad Publishing Company, 1989), loc. 32, Kindle.
20 hooks, *Teaching to Transgress*, 21, 120, 148–54.
21 E. J. Khantizan, W. E. McAuliffe, and K. S. Halliday, *Addiction and the Vulnerable Self: Modified Dynamic Group Therapy for Substance Abusers* (New York: The Guilford Press, 1990), loc. 196–207, Kindle.
22 Khantizan, McAuliffe, and Halliday, *Addiction and the Vulnerable Self*, loc. 196–207.
23 J. O. Prochaska, J. C. Norcross, and C. C. DiClemente, *Changing for Good* (New York: Harper Collins, 1994) (Kindle).
24 L. Pederson and C. S. Pederson, *The Expanded Dialectical Behavior Therapy Skills Training Manual: Practical DBT for Self-Help, and Individual and Group Treatment Settings* (Eau Claire, WI: Premier Publishing and Media, 2012) (Kindle).
25 https://learning-theories.com/situated-learning-theory-lave.html.
26 M. L. McCreary, J. J. Young, M. Y. Jones, J. E. Fife, and C. D. Pasquarello, "Project IMPPACT: A Psychoeducational Problem-Solving Intervention for Children," *Journal of Instructional Psychology* 38, no. 2 (2011): 124–32.

Chapter 5

1 As a pastoral psychotherapist I refer to six senses: sight, hearing, taste, touch, smell, and intuition (spirit).

2 L. Praglin, "The Nature of the 'In-Between' in D. W. Winnicott's Concept of Transitional Space and in Martin Buber's das Zwischenmenschliche," *Universitas* (2006): 1.

3 https://www.poetryfoundation.org/poems/147917/mr-roosevelt-regrets.

4 https://www.apa.org/pi/oema/resources/communique/2010/04/april-special.pdf.

5 https://www.apa.org/pi/oema/resources/communique/2010/04/april-special.pdf.

6 https://www.apa.org/pi/oema/resources/communique/2010/04/april-special.pdf.

7 https://www.psychologytoday.com/us/blog/witness/201301/the-best-predictor-future-behavior-is-past-behavior.

8 D. Augsburger, *Caring Enough to Confront* (Grand Rapids, MI: Baker Publishing Group, 2009) (Kindle). Augsburger stated that conflict is not inherently good or bad. Rather it is the approach that creates the difficulty. Augsburger suggested we care-front, that is we care to confront, and we confront in a caring manner.

9 V. E. Frankl, *Man's Search for Meaning* (Boston: Beacon Press, 1949) (Kindle), 76–77, 91–92.

10 The IMPPACT program was designed as a community-based program that applies salient dimensions of African American religiosity and cultural values in the effort to cultivate resilience and self-efficacy outcomes among African American families.

11 R. H. Barton, *Pursuing God's Will Together: A Discernment Practice for Leadership Groups* (Downers Grove, IL: Intervarsity Press, 2012) (Kindle).

12 https://dictionary.apa.org/mirror-technique.

13 The term "stopped out" is used for students who plan to return to school at a future time.

14 For a discussion on the importance of detoxification in the process of forgiveness, see E. L. Worthington Jr., *Forgiveness and Reconciliation: Theory and Application* (New York: Taylor & Francis, 2006).

15 Frankl, *Man's Search for Meaning*, 76–77.

16 D. W. Winnicott, *Playing and Reality* (New York: Routledge, 1971), 86.

Chapter 6

1 https://www.theatlantic.com/magazine/archive/1897/08/
strivings-of-the-negro-people/305446/; https://www.theatlantic.
com/magazine/archive/1965/11/w-e-b-dubois/660893/.
2 https://www.theatlantic.com/video/index/554972/web-dubois-
striving-negro/.
3 https://www.theatlantic.com/video/index/554972/web-dubois-
striving-negro/.
4 Clinical effective practices include therapeutic relationship and
alliance, agreement on counseling task, mutual acceptance of the
presenting problem, and agreement on processes and procedures.
5 This program includes components of social influence factors
(https://www.apa.org/international/united-nations/racism-
discrimination-comments.pdf); seeks to recast racial stress and
trauma ("Racial Trauma: Theory, Research, and Healing," special issue, *American Psychologist* 74, no. 1 (January 2019), ed.
L. Comas-Díaz, G. Nagayama Hall, H. A. Neville, and A. E.
Kazak); and addresses and incorporates the issue of distress (P.
P. Lui, "Racial Microaggression, Overt Discrimination, and Distress: (In) Direct Associations with Psychological Adjustment,"
The Counseling Psychologist 48, no. 4 (2020): 1–32).
6 F. E. Davis, *The Little Book of Race and Restorative Justice: Black
Lives, Healing, and US Social Transformation (Justice and Peace-
building)* (New York: Good Books, 2019) (Kindle).
7 For more on this approach, consult K. V. Hardy, "Healing the
Hidden Wounds of Racial Trauma," *Reclaiming Children and
Youth* 22, no. 1 (Spring 2013): 24–28.
8 J. P. Herrera-Escobar and J. C. Schneider, "From Survival to
Survivorship—Framing Traumatic Injury as a Chronic Condition," *New England Journal of Medicine* 387, no. 7 (2022): 581–83.
9 Philadelphia Adverse Childhood Experiences (ACES): https://
www.philadelphiaaces.org/philadelphia-ace-survey.

Chapter 7

1 This impression comes from experiencing her performances at
concerts and talking with members of the Berklee College of
Music community.

2 https://www.youtube.com/watch?v=qiT9lbw8rY4&list= RDqiT9lbw8rY4&start_radio=1.

3 L. Comas-Díaz, G. N. Hall, and H. A. Neville, "Racial Trauma Theory, Research, and Healing: Introduction to Special Issue," *American Psychologist* 74, no. 1 (2019): 1–5; Helms, Nicolas, and Green, "Racism and Ethnoviolence as Trauma: Enhancing Professional Training"; L. Comas-Dias, "Racial Trauma Recovery: A Race-Informed Therapeutic Approach to Racial Wounds," in *The Cost of Racism for People of Color: Contextualizing Experiences of Discrimination*, ed. A. N. Alvarez, C. T. H. Liang, and H. A. Neville (Washington, DC: American Psychological Association, 2016), 249–72.

4 A. Daugherty, *From Mindfulness to Heartfulness: A Journey of Trans-formation through the Science of Embodiment* (Bloomington: Balboa Press, 2014) (Kindle); M. Sockolov, *Practicing Mindfulness: 75 Essential Meditations to Reduce Stress, Improve Mental Health, and Find Peace in the Everyday* (Emeryville, CA: Althea Press, 2018) (Kindle).

5 R. G. Tedeschi, J. Shakespeare-Finch, K. Taku, and L. G. Calhoun, *Posttraumatic Growth: Theory, Research, and Application* (New York: Routledge, 2018), 147–50.

6 C. G. Jung, *Collected Works of C. G. Jung* (Princeton, NJ: Princeton University Press) (Kindle), 9.2: 8–10; Bye Blues, "Shadow Self: The Dark Side of Humanity?" Albawaba: Your Gateway to the Middle East (website), December 19, 2022, https://www.albawaba.com/editors-choice/shadow-self-dark-side-humanity-1502832.

7 Jung, *Collected Works of C. G. Jung*, 9.2: 8–10.

8 C. Cooper Jones, *Easy Beauty: A Memoir* (New York: Avid Reader Press/Simon & Schuster, 2022) (Kindle), 131–32.

9 https://www.poetryfoundation.org/poems/51642/invictus.

10 https://www.northwestern.edu/wellness/8-dimensions/spiritual-wellness.html.

11 E. H. Friedman, *The Myth of the Shiksa: And Other Essays* (New York: Seabury Books, 2008) (Kindle).

Conclusion

1 See Blackmon, *Slavery by Another Name*, 124; Wilkerson, *The Warmth of Other Suns*; Comas-Díaz et al., "Racial Trauma Theory,

Notes

Research, and Healing"; and Helms, Nicolas, and Green, "Racism and Ethnoviolence as Trauma."

2 Hannah-Jones, *The 1619 Project*; J. G. Ponterotto, J. M. Casas, L. A. Suzuki, and C. M. Alexander, *Handbook of Multicultural Counseling*, 2nd ed. (Thousand Oaks, CA: Sage, 2001); R. Takaki, *A Different Mirror: A History of Multicultural America* (Boston: Little, Brown, 1993).